D1587244

Fantastic Recipes from my
Favourite People

First published in Great Britain by Foxcote Books Ltd,
London 2006

A CIP catalogue record for this book is available from
the British Library

ISBN   1-905880-01-4
ISBN-13   978-1-905880-01-0

10 9 8 7 6 5 4 3 2 1

Designed and Typeset by Foxcote Books
Additional design by On Fire

Printed and bound in Germany by GGP Media GmbH,
Pössneck

www.foxcotebooks.com

Fantastic Recipes from my Favourite People

by

Poppy Fraser

illustrated by Leonora Grosvenor

foxcote

For my beloved husband, Henry

CONTENTS

'Without doubt, the worst cook I have ever come across.'
Henry Hughes, October 2004

It was lucky that my courtship with Henry was so brief as he had little time to experience my shocking culinary skills. I had learnt one recipe to perfection which looked and tasted as if it had been prepared by a master chef, and as with so many of the best recipes, actually took a few seconds to prepare. The few times I did cook for him, I prepared the same thing but he never seemed to notice or look in the fridge which contained only mayonnaise and an old bottle of dry white wine.

By the time we were married and living together, the role of cook was one that I had to assume. Henry would return home exhausted after a day in his wig and would be ravenous. I would try and rustle up something comforting. Within a week, I had poisoned him, and he lay groaning in bed after a simple plate of pasta with garlic and chillies. He became very worried for his future health, knowing the desperate truth that I had no idea how to make the simplest of things.

Despite not being able to cook, food is something that I think about morning, noon and night. This stems from having a father who lives to eat and an exceptionally good cook as a mother. My earliest memories are of the glorious, rich spread of teas that our nanny Diana would produce each day. The table would be covered in pancakes, scones, sandwiches, crisps, biscuits, shortbread and cakes, every single day. It was like a scene from Brambly Hedge and one that I looked forward to each day on returning from school. I remember going to visit cousins for tea and squealing in horror as we were offered healthy cucumber and marmite sandwiches and raw carrot sticks, never had I seen such desperate offerings. We were, in short, vastly spoilt and a nightmare for any host to have to deal with.

9

Later on at boarding school, whilst some were causing concern with their strange eating habits, I was busy heating up toastie machines in the French rooms and smuggling ingredients from the food hall. The staff grew wary of my greed and I was carefully watched so that I didn't receive more than my allotted one doughnut at tea. All of my pocket money was spent in the tuck shop, and I'd spend hours working out just what I could buy with my pennies.

When we discovered that I was expecting, the pressure to learn how to cook increased substantially. I had to get some help quickly. It was then that I thought of Auntie Ponnie's fantastic cook books which she wrote in the 1970s. The most famous of which, 'Lady Maclean's Cook Book' can be found covered in flour and sticky mess in many kitchens.

And so it is what I have gathered here in this little book. My kind family and friends have come to the rescue and given their favourite recipes. There are some corkers in here and a couple of very strange recipes, all of which I am very grateful for. I hope they will provide as much pleasure to you as they have to me.

Happy porking!

BREAKFAST

The Secret to Scrambled Eggs
Fritz von Westenholz

Fritz is charming, funny and a joy to spend time with.

Take a heavy bottomed pan and melt a good chunk of butter slowly in the pan. Shell your eggs, whisk and then... push them through a sieve into the butter.

This makes for the best scrambled eggs.

Lovat Breakfast Smoothie
Simon Lovat

My cousin Simon sent me this recipe just after a dramatic weekend in the Highlands when he was walking with friends and managed to lose my mother's treasured puppy Storm. She was found, by a miracle, after 24 hours by a bearded hillwalker, hence the 'long live Storm'.

2 bananas (over ripe if possible)
Half a punnet of raspberries
1 teaspoon of runny honey
Splash of milk
Generous helping of cream
Handful of ice

This is my perfect breakfast (for variation I sometimes add fresh mint or malt Ovaltine Lite...)

lots of love, and long live Storm.

Rosie's Rocket Fuel Porridge
Rosie Innes Ker

When not busy rushing around valuing Fabergé eggs for Sotheby's, Rosie stands on her head and performs extraordinarily impressive yogic positions. She needs to start the day with a bang, and this is what does it for her.

½ litre of water
Two large handfuls of jumbo oats
Six chopped (un-sulphured) apricots
A handful of raisins
½ tablespoon of honey

Measure the water in a pan and immediately add the oats before putting on the stove. Porridge heats up very fast and should be stirred constantly. Add the dried fruit as you stir. You can add any combination you like, but I would not advise using orange apricots. (They should be condemned to hell along with anything pickled and coriander.) Un-sulphured apricots have a wonderful honey flavour. When the consistency is right add the honey to sweeten and tuck in.

15

'A Tolly'
James Tollemache

Have you ever tried to make a fried egg sandwich? If not, let me tell you it is no simple affair!

The main problems are crumbly toast, so the runny yolk falls through the middle, as well as only ever getting an odd bite with yolk, and when you *do* get a bit of yolk, it invariably spills out over the side or down your chin onto your clean shirt!

Therefore, my recipe to you is:

A piece of very cheap white bread. The best is Mother's Pride, but ask your local prep school for the latest version. This bread, due to its rubbery composition, does not crumble!

Spreadable butter – so as not to rip the toast when spreading eggs in rows on the toast and serve...

...Quails' eggs!

This means that with every mouthful you can have a bit with yolk in. Also due to the size of quails' eggs, there is limited spilling of yolk.

Altogether it is delicious and can be called: 'A Tolly'.

Simon and Tommy's Scrambled Eggs for Breakfast
Simon and Tommy Soros

*This rather charming and unusual recipe comes from my cousin
Flora Fraser's wee children. When asked for a recipe this is what they
came up with.*

'Hey, let's make scrambled eggs.
Eggs, that's what we need. Six.
Slimy and yellow in the bowl.
Hey, let's beat them up.
They're all scrambled up.
Then we cook it.
Slowly. Heavy. Very yellow.
Let's eat it.'

With love from Flora, 19 May 2005

Wheat Free Muesli
Rosalind Portman

Mrs Portman is an incredibly impressive woman who won a prestigious Beacon Award in 2004 for setting up the Family Links' Nurturing Programme, working through schools to develop relationship skills and improve children's behaviour and achievements in the classroom. It offers parallel parenting education for their families. The programme is designed to help prevent bullying, antisocial behaviour, child abuse, truancy and juvenile crime.

4 cups of organic porridge oats
1 cup of sunflower seeds
1 cup of pumpkin seeds
3 cups of linseed
1 cup of chopped dates
1 cup of sultanas
1 cup of chopped apricots
1 cup of chopped hazelnuts, almonds or walnuts
Optional - a cup of broken up Millet rice made by Nature's Earth.

Chopped prunes are also good as an addition, or as a substitute for another dried fruit. Store in the fridge when made up.

This is a cereal which works very well eaten with cranberry, apple or pineapple juice.

Allow lots of time to chew the nuts and seeds!

CANAPES

Humous
Momin Latif

We last saw Momin when, after a month of touring round India, we arrived in Delhi, where he lives. Out of the sweat, dust and endless chapatis and daal, Momin appeared like a vision from heaven – or at least like a very jolly deity who has enjoyed a great deal of good food and laughter. We were ushered through an Aladdin's cave of collected treasures into his bedroom where Momin greeted us, his ample frame contained in a pure white kurti, stretched over a giant white four-poster bed, beckoning chilled champagne and this delicious humous. Momin identifies what is best and simplest, and this was one of the most memorable and rejuvenating meals of my life. This recipe is simply the definitive humous and is best eaten cold, preferably on a very hot day with a glass of something crisp and dry.

Soak overnight one cup of dried chick peas with a teaspoon of baking powder which softens them.

The very next day, add one litre of water, two teaspoons of salt and two garlic cloves. Bring to the boil and then simmer for an hour.

Drain from the liquid but keep behind half a cup full of water.

Magimix them, add the juice of a lemon, six tablespoons of tahini and two cloves of garlic.

Put into an attractive bowl with some chopped parsley, some olive oil and a sprinkling of chilli.

Bruschetta
Mary Fellowes

Mary dashes around working for Vogue *and going to parties and has little time to spend cooking. She used to live with Will Young and would feed this to him before he went off to his* Pop Idol *auditions, as it can be made in a trice and is fortifying.*

Toast Poilane bread.

Fry it in infused olive oil – either sun-dried tomato or basil – any Mediterranean flavour will do.

Place upon a serving dish and add chopped small vine or cherry tomatoes, sun-dried tomatoes and handfuls of rocket and baby spinach, lots of herb salt and fresh basil and ground black pepper.

Keep in a warming oven for ten minutes prior to serving and, just before serving, throw on handfuls of shaved parmesan.

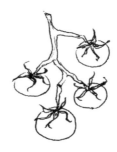

Chorizo Nibbles
Rose Astor

Rose set up BUSY KIDS LONDON, which provides incredible courses for children such as cooking, photography, yoga and storytelling. A complete life-saver for parents and more fun than anything else offered for children that I could find.

I was inspired by this as alternative to crisps and peanuts before dinner.

1 chorizo sliced in ½cm pieces
Half a bottle of red wine (use the one left over from dinner the night before that would otherwise sit by the cooker forever)

Put tiny amount of olive oil in a big saucepan.
Toss and sweat the chorizo off on a high heat.
Pour in red wine and simmer for one hour until the chorizo has absorbed all the wine.

Serve delicious and hot!

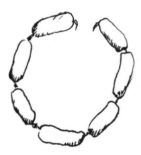

Goat's Cheese Parcels with Red Onion Marmalade
Zara Noel

One of the luckiest things ever to happen to me was to be placed in a bedroom with Zara when I first went off to boarding school. We've been inseparable ever since.

1 roll of goat's cheese
1 packet of filo pastry sheets
2 large red onions
2 cups of red wine
3 large tablespoons of redcurrant jelly
Rocket

Grease a baking tray.

To make the red onion marmalade: Finely chop the onions and sweat in a frying pan. Once the onions are soft, pour in the red wine, add the redcurrant jelly and simmer until the wine has reduced to make the red onions look like a marmalade.

To make the filo parcels: Place the square sheets of filo pastry on the greased baking tray: I use two sheets so that they don't split. Place a slice of goat's cheese in the centre and then spoon in two tablespoons of the red onion marmalade.
Bring together the corners of the filo pastry and twist so it forms a small parcel.
If there is a large amount of excess pastry at the top, cut it off.
Repeat the above for each parcel.
Before placing in the oven, brush with egg white which helps to crisp up the pastry.
Place in the oven at 180°C for ten minutes, the filo parcels should be turning a golden brown.

Carefully loosen them from the baking tray and place on a bed of rocket.

Peppers di Padron
Eddie Hart

Eddie is like a little teddy bear with sparkling eyes. His party trick, which he performs in any situation, is his forward roll. He is the owner of one of the best restaurants in London. Fino's serves the most delicious tapas that you could ever hope to find. Far, far better than Spain's version. I spent my honeymoon in Andalusia and hunted around for food to match what I'd known from Fino's but alas to no avail.

These are the best little peppers, they come in a bag and one in every forty is exceedingly hot. Gently fry them in a little olive oil for about three minutes until the skin begins to blister. Put on a dish and sprinkle with sea salt and eat immediately.

Paté Waghorn
Dave Ker

Dave is one of the funniest people you will ever hope to meet.

½lb pig liver
1 apple
1 onion
1 clove of garlic
¼ tsp pepper
1 tsp salt
4 anchovy fillets
3 bacon
Cayenne

Put all ingredients through a mincer (having chopped bacon first).
Add 2oz butter, 1oz flour and ¼ pint milk to sauce. Add 1 beaten
egg and bake in a greased oven proof dish for one hour, gas 4 or
180°C.

Smoked Mackerel Paté
Pepi Hughes

Henry's mother has always made this and it knocks the spots off any bought version. Easy, fresh and delicious.

Some smoked mackerel
Juice of one lemon
A tub of Marscapone cheese, Philadelphia or crème fraiche, it simply doesn't matter which

Add all of the ingredients to the magimix, whizz around for a few seconds.

Spread it onto oatcakes, or warm toast.

Everyone always loves this.

STARTERS

Crab Croquettes
The Countess of Dalhousie

These are very versatile and are ideal to eat on a picnic, as a starter, or even as a canapé.

3oz plain flour
3oz butter
6½oz fish stock or milk
8oz crab meat
1 tablespoon of anchovy essence
1 tablespoon of chopped parsley

Melt butter, add flour, mix together on heat. Add liquid and stir until mixture thickens. Add crab meat, anchovy essence and parsley.

Leave to cool and, when cool, shape into croquettes, dip in flour and egg and then dried bread crumbs. Deep fry.

Smoked Sausage Starter
HRH The Duchess of Cornwall

I am very grateful for this mouth-watering starter.

1 smoked sausage
1lb field mushrooms
1 pint of double cream
Black pepper

Chop sausage into slices.
Slice peeled mushrooms.
Place in oven proof dish in layers.
Add cream, add black pepper.
Put in medium oven for 25 minutes.

Oeufs Czernin
Cecilia McEwan

Cecilia sent me this recipe whilst she was in Austria, I made them immediately and nearly had a cardiac arrest they were so good.

Take one egg per person:

Separate yolks and whites.
Mix yolks with grated cheese, any white cheese ie parmesan or cheddar etc.
Mix until really thick, adding pepper and salt. Put in the fridge. Cut rounds of sliced bread, 3-3½ inches wide, deep fry on one side only and leave. Before cooking, place yolk mixture on cooked side of bread. Mix egg whites until stiff, pile this on the top of the egg mixture, like a meringue. Cook in hot oil in a deep fat fryer until bread is brown on other side. Also cook curly parsley at the end in the fryer, briefly, until crisp, scatter over the meringue – it looks and tastes very good.

Onion Tart
The Marchioness of Salisbury

Hannah thought that this should be called Kevin's Onion Tart but others have named it Farty Onion Tart. She describes it as being dynamite. When her husband was young, his parents believed in starvation being the answer to illness and Hannah once found one of his siblings eating her dog food in the back of the car!

3 medium onions
2 cloves garlic
1 small leek
2 tablespoons chives
2 spring onions
1 teaspoon brown sugar
Splash of red wine
Salt / pepper
2oz butter and teaspoon olive oil
½lb grated Ashmore cheese (similar to strong cheddar)

Pastry:
1lb plain flour
½lb butter
1 egg
Teaspoon dry basil

For the pastry: combine flour, butter and basil to form a crumb mixture. Make a well in the centre, and add the egg. Start to mix, then add a little water, just enough to combine into a dough. Place in fridge for half an hour.

Place butter and oil in pan, put on low heat. Slice onions, leek, garlic and spring onions and add to pan. Cook on a low heat. Add the sugar, keep mixing until the onions start to turn golden brown. Add the wine to de-glaze. The mixture should be moist (if not add more butter) mix in one tablespoon of the chives and salt and pepper to taste.

(continued...)

Roll out the pastry thinly and roll it onto a 10" – 12" square tray. Fork the pastry and bake at 200°C until golden brown. Sprinkle half the grated cheese over the pastry and then spread the onion mixture on top. Sprinkle the rest of the cheese over the tart, put back in the oven and cook for a further ten minutes at 200°C.

Once cooked, sprinkle the remainder of the chives on top.

Ideal for shoots, picnics or even as a lunch starter.

Onion Tart

Chicken Liver Salad
Fiona Allen

My Aunt Fiona lives in Tuscany and says that there are hardly any recipes in Italy as the ingredients all taste so good as they are. Lucky, lucky Fiona.

This recipe is so simple and easy and it will suit any situation, outside for a picnic in the summer, or as an easy dinner with a group of friends.

200-250g chicken livers
10 leaves of fresh sage
4 slices of streaky bacon, cut into small pieces
1 soft round lettuce
Oil, vinegar, salt and pepper

Wash and dry the lettuce, tear the leaves into pieces and put in a bowl with a vinaigrette dressing.

Slice the chicken livers into three or four pieces (having separated them from the hearts, if sold together).

Heat some olive oil in a small frying pan, and when hot, put in the sage leaves and the liver pieces. Be careful, as they will spit. Fry quickly, turning often for a couple of minutes only. Pour the whole thing over the salad.

Serve warm with crusty bread.

If you do not have fresh sage, then fry the bacon pieces until crisp, and add to the salad with the livers instead.

Prawn Robin
Mrs Raoul Lempriere Robin

My great Aunt Sheelagh lives in Jersey in an ancient house where nothing has changed for the last hundred years. Although one enters the kitchen, and indeed the dining room, with a mixture of trepidation over what you might discover lurking somewhere, the food is always perfectly delicious when it finally arrives. My Great Uncle Raoul was an exceptional cook and was famed for his jugged hare dish which took three days to prepare. Aunt Sheelagh now lives there alone – as constant and unchanging as the house, and her recipes evoke the magic of lost summers in a bygone age.

2lb prawns
2 sherry glasses of sherry
2oz butter
2 small pots of cream
2 egg yolks

Melt the butter and cook prawns in it until done, add sherry and boil for five minutes. Whip up cream with yolks and add it to the prawns twenty minutes before serving. DO NOT BOIL. You can add a cup of cooked rice or serve it separately.

This is enough for six people.

Kipastata
Sue Phipps

Sue is married to Auntie Ponnie's son Jeremy and is one of the world's leading equestrian artists. Extremely well exhibited, Susan Crawford has painted most of the world's great horses.

Very healthy and can be made the day before!

3 packets of kipper fillets (fresh or frozen)
2 leeks
1 red onion

French dressing:
Olive oil (3 parts)
Balsamic vinegar (1 part)
Lemon juice
Brown sugar or honey
Whole grain mustard
Black pepper and salt

Strip skin off back of fillets, and cut into strips. Chop leeks and cook, and cut up onion into thin rings.

Marinate kippers in dressing overnight.

Lay out artistically on a sheet with leeks and onion rings… and there you are!

Baked Eggs
Harry Lopes

Not a very well known cook, Harry is the slowest eater. When everyone else is on their coffee, Harry is just about to finish his starter.

This is a starter which everyone enjoys but is incredibly easy to do.

A baking tray
Cocotte dish
Free range eggs
Butter
Double cream
Salt & pepper
Lea & Perrins and / or Ketchup (optional)

You put one or two eggs in the cocotte dish with a small knob of butter and a tablespoon of cream. Season well.

Put the cocotte dish in a baking tray filled with enough cold water to come two thirds of the way up the dishes. Put in the oven gas mark 5 for 20-25 minutes or until just set; hard on the outside, soft on the inside.

An optional extra is the Lea & Perrins and / or Ketchup. A few drops of these sink towards the bottom.

Puff Pastry Tart with Caramelised Onions, Roasted Tomatoes and Goat's Cheese
Alice Lutyens

Alice is ruthlessly efficient in the kitchen and I always eat incredibly well at her house. She also said that this book would be more politically correct if it included a recipe from a deaf person. She is one of my greatest friends.

Serves 4

1 pack ready-made puff pastry – the one already rolled out is best!
6 large red onions
1 pack cherry tomatoes
1 pack goats cheese – you need a soft-ish one. The ones that are spreadable cook best I think
50g butter
1 teaspoon of white sugar
2 tbs olive oil
1 tbs balsamic vinegar
Pinch dried oregano
Salt and pepper

Switch the oven to 200°C

Slice the onions. It is not necessary to slice them very finely – quite large slices are fine (each one being the size and shape of an orange segment, perhaps). Melt the butter in a large frying pan, then cook the onions over a low heat for roughly thirty minutes, until they are very soft. You don't want them to be brown, just really sticky and gooey. Add more butter if needed.

While the onions are cooking, slice the tomatoes length-wise, place them in a roasting tin and throw them around in the olive oil and balsamic vinegar. Then turn them all so the sliced side is

(continued...)

facing upwards, and sprinkle the sugar, oregano, salt and pepper over them. Roast until quite brown around the edges (about twenty minutes).

Roll the pastry out onto a lightly floured baking tray, and score the pastry about 1cm from the edge. This will mean the pastry rises around the edges. Prick the inner pastry with a fork, then pile the caramelised onions on top, within the scored edges. Brush some melted butter around the edges. Scatter the tomatoes and chunks of goat's cheese all over, then put in the oven for about twenty minutes, until the pastry is puffed and golden.

This is still very yum cold the next day…

Tomato Mousse
Sarah Lopes

7 fluid ounces tomato juice
7 fluid ounces tomato pulp (liquidised or sieved)
1 tablespoon Worcestershire Sauce
Salt and pepper
Gelatine (1 packet + 5 tablespoons boiling water)
4 ounces double cream (whipped till stiff)
4 ounces single cream

Mix together tomatoes, seasoning and gelatine. Allow to nearly set, mix with whipped cream and allow to set and chill. Can be spiced up with Tabasco or Chilli powder.

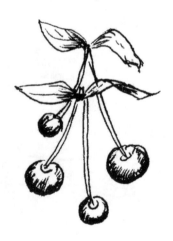

Pressed Bacon on a Bed of Sweetcorn Surprise
Wenty Beaumont

Wenty's grandfather had a party trick of getting the iron out when he was entertaining and pressing the bacon before serving to his guests. This is one of my favourite recipes from the book and I only wish there were more people like him around today – ironed bacon will always be remembered, while who can distinguish between the sea of smart canapés that are served so endlessly at parties nowadays?

Place bacon in a warm buttered baking tray, ensuring that some butter is also smeared on top of the bacon. Place an old iron, preferably pre-1970s, on the hottest hob available. Leave iron until as hot as is physically possible. When the iron is literally red hot, remove it from the hot hob and press down on top of the bacon. Gently iron the bacon in the same way you would iron the collar of a shirt, applying more butter to encourage crispiness.

The pressed bacon should be served on a small bed of sweetcorn surprise. Warm, drained sweetcorn, flavoured with a light drizzling of blue dragon sweet chilli sauce. Soy sauce is also a suitable addition to this, as is ketchup and mayonnaise.

To complete, cook a fried egg in the bacon juice and place on top of the bacon, which should by this stage be on top of the steaming sweetcorn surprise.

Fig Bundles
Clare Kerr

Clare is so health conscious that she boils her vegetables in mineral water. She is about the most organised person you could ever meet and is an environmental strategy consultant for the Conservative Party.

Serves 6

6 ripe figs
6 thin slices of Parma ham
100g soft goat's cheese, ricotta or gorgonzola
Rocket leaves
Extra virgin olive oil
Balsamic vinegar
Salt and pepper
6 walnuts

Heat the oven to 200°C / gas mark 5.
Crisscross the top of each fig to two-thirds of the way down.
Squeeze the base of the figs to open them a little.
Spoon the cheese into the centre of the figs.
Add a pinch of salt and pepper.
Wrap each fig in a thin slice of Parma ham, place on a baking tray.

Cook for 5-10 minutes until the Parma ham has just begun to crisp and the cheese has begun to melt.
Serve each fig on a bed of rocket.
Drizzle with olive oil and balsamic.
Further ideas: add a walnut to the cheese stuffing prior to heating the figs in the oven; use honey & lemon dressing instead of balsamic.

Pheasant Starter
Tessa Keswick

My aunt Tessa is one of the most inherently cool people I know, witty stylish and ahead of her time.

(for four people – double the quantities for more)

2 young pheasants
3oz streaky bacon
1lb tin of chestnuts

Roast the pheasants covered with the bacon for forty minutes or until cooked. At the same time heat the chestnuts through in butter in a pan.

Carve the pheasants into pieces and in a serving dish place chestnuts in the bottom with the breast meat on top and the legs around the dish.

Sauce:
Half a pint of cream
1 tbls Worcestershire sauce
1 tbls of mushroom sauce or Harvey's essence
1 teaspoon anchovy essence
1 tbls brandy and salt and pepper

Cook sauce for ten minutes until thickened and pour over the pheasant. Then chop up the bacon and sprinkle over and finally add some parsley.

SOUPS

Avelia's "ZUPPA DI LENTICCHIE"
Stefano Massimo

Stefano is an incredibly talented photographer whose beautiful daughter Violante was one of our bridesmaids.

Avelia Gasperini is a lovely old lady from the village where I have a house in the country near Roma. She is almost eighty and still tends her own vegetable and fruit garden in the valley below the village, walking up and down the steep hill every day. Practically all she eats she grows herself. The only allowance for modernity is her freezer which she regularly stocks with her own produce as it comes into season. As a result she is as fit as a fiddle.

500g of small brown lentils. In Roma I use the tiny lentils from the islands of Ponza or Ventotene which are legendary. Here you can find French puy, Italian castelluccio or Spanish lenteja Pardina lentils by La Asturiana (If in London, buy them from a Spanish butcher shop called City Meat in King's Road SW3, near World's End.) All three are good substitutes.

2 or 3 celery sticks (if possible with their leaves)
Italian unsmoked pancetta (City Meat), three thickly cut rashers, cut in cubes
Onion – 1 large one, chopped
Garlic – 1, 2 or 3 cloves, depending on your taste, chopped
400g chopped or peeled tomatoes (only use fresh tomatoes when in season, do not EVER use those virtual reality tomatoes from countries like Holland that taste of nothing because they have never seen the sun and are grown with dubious techniques)
Tinned Italian tomatoes are infinitely better because they have been allowed to ripen naturally in the Mediterranean sun and canned immediately
Chillies – 1 or 2 tiny strong dry ones, crushed.
Sea Salt

46

(continued...)

The lentils above are so tender they don't need preliminary cooking. If you want, you can soak them in advance.

Fry the cubed pancetta in a little extra virgin olive oil until most of the fat has melted but not all, then add the chopped onion and garlic. Let the onion sweat on a low heat (you can cover pan if you want) making sure that you don't frazzle the pancetta and burn the onion. Stir the mixture so that it does not stick. Add the lentils and plenty of water. Add salt to taste (depending on the saltiness of the pancetta). Break the celery (or chop roughly) in pieces and add to the soup. Lentils expand enormously so make sure you check as they are cooking, adding water as necessary. The cooking time should be around half an hour. This soup is better eaten the next day as all the flavours will have had the time to infuse. Drizzle on some very good extra virgin olive oil (cold pressed).

You can modify this dish into "PASTA E LENTICCHIE" by adding extra water and a little salt, bringing to the boil and adding Mezzi Tubetti Pasta (half tubes) or spaghetti snapped in lengths of four or five centimetres.

The perfect bread to accompany this zuppa is the classic Poilane from their bakery in Elizabeth Street in London. This bread is the closest I have found here in Britain to the Pane Casareccio I used to eat as a child and still do in Lazio.

In Europe there are three countries I know of that understand the art of breadmaking: Italy, France and Germany.

Wedding Soup
Drogo Montague

This recipe comes from the Swiss ski resort of Klosters.
It was designed for pregnant women in the middle of winter to give them a creamy, rich soup on freezing winter days. It is delicious.

30g fine diced smoked bacon
10g butter
10g fine diced shallots
60g fine diced celery
60g fine diced carrot
60g fine diced leek
5 decilitre chicken stock
1 decilitre double cream

A 300g piece of smoked bacon

Put the piece of smoked bacon in the chicken stock and reduce by one third.
Sweat off all the fine diced vegetables in the butter till softened.
Once the chicken stock has reduced by one third discard the piece of bacon.
Add the bacon flavoured chicken stock to the vegetables and bring to the boil.
Add the double cream and reduce on a gentle heat for five minutes.
Season to taste.
Blitz the soup with a hand-held blender till it has a good foam on top (this will make the soup lighter and look good).

Summer Pea Soup
Vicky Orr Ewing

½ or ¾lb of peas
1 potato
1 onion
1 pint of stock
½ pint of double cream
Juice of ½ lemon

Put the peas, tatties, onion and half the stock in a pan, bring to a boil. Cover and simmer for fifteen minutes.
Put in a blender and puree.
Return to pan and add the remaining stock and simmer for five minutes.

Add cream and lemon juice, salt and pepper.

Tania's Borsch
Tania Illingworth

Tania is descended from Leo Tolstoy, and when her great-grandparents fled the revolution in 1918 they came to England with the family jewels sewn into the swaddling clothes of her grandmother.

Boil raw beetroots until not entirely soft. Cool and peel the skins off.

Liquidise (chop them up first) completely in Kenwood (magimix is no good).

Add Lea and Perrins, tomato ketchup, dash of balsamic vinegar, salt and pepper, touch of sugar, a Knorr cube.

Taste. Add spoon greek yogurt or crème fraiche, milk or cream for taste.

Consistency should be 'easy pouring' but not like milk.

TO SERVE COLD
Put blob of sour cream and chives on top.

TO SERVE HOT
Put blob of cream on top (if you pour the cream over the back of a spoon slowly, it does not disappear into the soup but stays on top).

Another recipe to be served hot from under the grill or at room temperature:

Thickly slice same cooked and boiled beetroots. Slice thick goat's cheese on top of each round slice. Put under grill until sizzling.

Serve on bed of rocket or salad with generous dribble of balsamic vinegar (the best) on top.

Vichyoisse
Vicky Orr Ewing

6 leeks
4 tbls butter
4 tatties
1 ½ pints of stock
½ pint of double cream
Chives

Cut the white parts of the leeks in butter till soft but don't brown them.

Peel and slice the tatties and add to the leeks with stock, salt and pepper and some grated nutmeg to taste. Simmer until all the vegetables are cooked.

Blend until smooth, chill. Add the cream and chives before serving.

Roasted Pumpkin and Onion Soup
John and Helen Bond, The Duke of Wellington Public House.

Central London is full of minimalist, soulless eateries where the managers are unnecessarily grand and overcharge for their tasteless food. Fortunately, nestling in Belgravia lies the haven of the Duke of Wellington pub where, for many years, John and Helen Bond, the Irish Landlords, greeted everyone by name and made everyone feel at home.

I often used to sit by the fire and watch the same old regulars, including Holly, a mongrel who has the softest fur that I have ever stroked – the secret of this being her daily treat of an ashtray full of bitter.

Chicken stock cube
Water
Pumpkin
Spring onion
Large onions
Shallots
Thyme
Pinch all purpose seasoning
Salt and pepper

Bake all chopped vegetables and spices in olive oil. Add to water and stock. Simmer for 20 minutes and then puree.

MAIN COURSE
(MEAT)

Sienna's Lemon Roast Chicken
Sienna Miller

I get hysterical about cooking chicken as I can't bear a dried-out carcass, quite revolting. This clever little massaged chick always comes out juicy and tasty.

Chop fresh thyme and sage and mix with lemon juice, salt, pepper and olive oil.

Lift the skin of the chicken up and stuff underneath, place skin back into position with skewers or string. Gently massage oil on the top of the skin.

Take half an onion and half of the lemon (left over from squeezing) and place inside the chicken. Cover with olive oil, lemon juice, salt and pepper. Cook at 180°C for an hour and a half, depending on the size of the chicken. Leave to stand for fifteen minutes.

For the gravy:
Use the sauces from the roasting try, drain off remaining oil. Add the juice of a lime, a dash of soya sauce, half a cup of white wine, some Bisto chicken gravy granules and some of the water used to steam the vegetables.

Season to taste and cook until the sauce thickens.

Shepherd's Pie or Cottage Pie
Anthony Cazalet

One of my most favourite meals is Cottage Pie.

This quintessentially English dish is vital to surviving a harsh winter. After having spent a morning outside in frosty, crunchy fields, nothing excites me more than returning home to open the oven and see the bubbling glorious Bolognese sauce rising up through the creamy mash. Tucking in to a steaming plate full of runny pie with a generous squirting of ketchup and peas is my idea of complete heaven.

Nothing will beat the pie when it is done well although very few people have the knack and yet it should be so simple. So often the mash is plain and disgusting and the meat lacking in any flavour.

Anthony Cazalet is a bon viveur who lives at Rose Cottage with Letty his Staffordshire bull terrier. Rose Cottage is somewhere where the door is always open, and the 'flying turd' as he likes to call Letty, leaps from lap to lap. I have enjoyed the greatest of pies, eaten long into the afternoon accompanied by never ending glasses of fine red wine and Anthony's inimitable tummy-shaking laugh. He is fantastically relaxed about cooking, as one should be, and has given this brilliant recipe.

Many people would like to claim they make the best pie. It would be foolish, at best, for me make such a claim as it can be a rather a hit and miss affair. I have always felt that the Cottage pie is made with beef and the Shepherd's, surprisingly, lamb. This recipe is usually carried out with lamb but beef could be just as easily substituted.

I have no concept of quantities and usually end up making too much which is of no consequence as it freezes well.

Into a square sided deep frying pan put some oil and fry up a diced onion or two, depending on size. With a hot pan put in the

(continued...)

meat, say a pound and a half of minced lamb and make certain it is broken up and browned all over.

At this stage I like to add some 'action' to liven up the meat that would otherwise be rather dull. Worcestershire sauce, two large chopped chillies (not too hot and skin only) three or four cloves of garlic (chopped not crushed) a good ⅓ of a bottle of red wine (good, within reason) and some tomato paste or tabasco if that is your fancy. At this stage if you need some bulk and like the colour add some diced carrots.

With the pan covered this can simmer away for a happy hour or two. At this stage you are supposed to take any fat off the top, if you can be bothered. Equally if you have bought good lean mince it will matter little.

Boil some skinned potatoes until they are soft. Mash them with your favoured implement and put in ¼lb of butter and a quantity of cream until it is of a suitable consistency. While stirring add salt pepper and ground nutmeg to taste. I like a large bit of pepper and Maldon salt but that is being a bit picky.

In a dish put the meat and cover with the mash. Roughly half and half is a good proportion but if in doubt add more meat. Sprinkle some grated parmesan cheese on the mash and heat it up before serving.

These pies were meant to use up left-overs, and there is a school that prefers chunks of meat rather than mince. It is important to keep the pie slightly runny and stock can be added if necessary. I cannot be bothered to make stock and so usually add more wine if it is drying up.

Gina's "POLPETTE" (Meatballs)
Stefano Massimo

Gina Ortenzi was my father's housekeeper when I was a child in the Lazio countryside and practically brought me up. She used to make these polpette for me and my best friend, her son Angelo, who was only two months older than me and is still close to me today. I loved her very much and whenever I eat them I cannot help but think of her.

1 kg of minced beef
3 eggs
Nutmeg (⅓ of a nut, grated)
Big bunch of flat leaf parsley, chopped
Grated rind of 2 unwaxed lemons
2 garlic cloves, finely chopped
3 slices of Poilane bread, if poss. or stale farmhouse bread, soaked in milk and then squeezed out and crumbled to the consistency of the minced meat
Salt & pepper

Mix all the ingredients with your hands and make sure that the mixture is properly amalgamated. Make little meat balls with your hands (4 or 5cm in diameter) rolling the meat around your palms. Shallow fry in olive oil.

This amount should make 35 meatballs in all:

Men: 7 a head   Women: 6 a head

Gina always used beef and parsley but they could be made with lamb and chopped mint.

Serve with a salad of Rucola (we call it Rughetta in Roma) and / or mixed leaves dressed with a simple vinaigrette: 1 measure of white wine vinegar or lemon juice.

(continued...)

3 measures of good extra virgin olive oil
Salt, pepper & a little sugar
Dijon mustard to taste
Shake the vinaigrette before dressing the salad which should be
thoroughly mixed before serving.

Five Hour Lamb
Kate Goldsmith

Quite nice to bung this in the oven and forget about it, as it takes so long to cook, and will taste better the longer it is left once cooked.

Serves 5

1 large leg of lamb
1 bunch of rosemary
1 bunch of thyme
4 large potatoes chunkily cut
4 large carrots chunkily cut
3 large onions quartered
1 large sweet potato chunkily cut
5 whole cloves of garlic
8 rashers of smoky bacon
1 bottle of white wine
1 good glug of olive oil
Salt
Pepper

The first thing to do is brown the leg of lamb on all sides in the olive oil, then put the lamb on a plate to one side. Using the same pan, fry the onions in a little more olive oil, once soft and golden add the bacon and garlic. Once the bacon is cooked (not crispy), add your herbs and give a good stir, fry all that for one minute to infuse with the herbs. Then add all your vegetables in no particular order – toss them about and cook for five minutes. Then nestle the lamb back into the pan with the vegetables carefully arranged around it, add the whole bottle of wine and then another wine bottle full of water. Bring all this to the boil and then cover very tightly and place in the low heat oven (140°C) for five hours. Once ready it may be necessary to spoon a little fat off the surface, add your salt and pepper now. Serve straight from the pot with bread and green beans.

Raka Taka Ribs a la Mungai
Vinnie Day

Vinnie was brought up in the Kenyan bush and has become a very successful jewellery designer. She ate this throughout her childhood alongside the wild animals who are sent crazy by the smells of the ribs sizzling in their tin.

Pork ribs
Olive oil
Handful of fresh thyme
Tinned tomatoes
Dollop of honey
Dash of Lea and Perrins
Splash of tabasco

Whip up the marinade: chuck tomatoes with honey, thyme, Lea and Perrins and for the hot-mouthed, tabasco. Add salt and pepper. Leave the ribs in the marinade for as long as possible.

Prepare the oven, or fire if you're in the bush.

Cook the ribs in a tin with all the marinade for half an hour. Keep the marinade for extra taste. Serve with mashed potato and crunchy salad.

Chicken Biryani
Aatish Taseer

Aatish was taught this by an ancient cook who was terrified that, not knowing how to cook anything else, he would starve to death at university.

Butter
Basmati rice
Ghee (clarified butter)
3 medium onions diced
1 kg chicken, skinned and cut up into parts
6 large garlic cloves, crushed
Ginger, 2 inch piece crushed
10 cloves
2 big black cardamoms
Cinnamon
Bay leaf
Red chilli powder
Turmeric
Salt
Plain yoghurt
Garam masala
Biryani powder (if available)
2-3 fresh green chillies
1 cup tomato juice
Saffron diluted in a cup of milk, if wanted

Put two tablespoons of ghee into a medium sized pot with two tablespoons of butter. Add onions to pot on a medium flame. Crush garlic and ginger in a mortar and add as paste.

Then add cloves, cardamom, cinnamon and bay leaf. Cook spices until onions brown, then add ½ teaspoon turmeric, 1-2 spoon red chilli, 3 spoons salt. Add chicken and let it cook in the spices for about ten minutes on a medium-light flame. When chicken is

(continued...)

covered with spices and the fragrance of the spices starts to rise, add 2-3 tablespoons yoghurt and stir it in, add garam masala and biryani powder.

Cover the pot and let chicken cook on a low flame for twenty minutes, checking it frequently.

Add water if needed, the sauce should be thick and on level with the meat, though not covering it entirely. Separately start to boil rice, making sure it is slightly under-cooked.

Then take a large pot and put another tablespoon of clarified butter in before adding a generous layer of the semi-cooked rice. Add a layer of chicken over that, two more tablespoons of yoghurt, the tomato juice and the saffron in milk if wanted. Then add the rest of the rice to create another layer. Place a tea towel on the edge of the pot and cover it with a lid, letting it cook for 20-30 minutes on an extremely low flame.

Serve with raita or even plain yoghurt.

63

Torie's Lunchtime Lancashire Hot Pot
Torie Legge Bourke

Torie once owned a Shitzu called Hu Flung Dung, known as Huey.

For six greedy people

Scrag end of lamb, or lamb leg chops – allow about two chops per person or equivalent in lamb pieces (best to have meat on the bone to improve flavour while cooking). People usually want second helpings. Think greedy. Trim off excess fat and any tough skin.

4 large potatoes – peeled and sliced (about ½ cm thick or slightly thinner) can be done night before and kept in bowl of water
2 medium onions – peeled and sliced and rings separated. Pre-prepare as for potatoes
6 lambs' kidneys – halved and de-veined, can be prepared the night before and kept in the fridge
Handful of dried barley
2 bay leaves
Teaspoon of dried mixed herbs
2 pints beef or chicken stock
Olive oil
Salt and pepper

Rush into the kitchen. Heat the oven to 350°F ie medium hot.

Take a large, heavy, lidded casserole dish (such as Le Creuset or similar) oil well with some of the olive oil.

Lay the slices of approx two of the potatoes in a fan shape to cover base of the casserole in a single layer. Lay on top of a layer of chops or meat pieces to cover the potatoes pretty completely. Sprinkle over half the mixed herbs, one baby leaf, a good pinch of salt and a scrunch of fresh black pepper and half the onion rings. Lay on top of them half the kidneys, and sprinkle over half the barley.

(continued...)

Repeat with another layer of meat, herbs, onions, seasoning, kidneys and barley. This should fill the dish to within about one inch of the top.

Make up two pints or more of stock and pour over the layered meat. If using cubes, use three cubes for two pints (ie half a cube more than usual per pint – helps to improve the flavour). Stock should come up level with top layer of meat / veg mixture.

Cover the whole dish with another layer of interlocking potato slices so that the meat is completely covered – you can add slices into the centre etc to make a 'hat' of the slices as you cover the meat. Brush (or drizzle over) more olive oil to lightly coat the potatoes.

Cover tightly with lid or if that's gone missing at the back of the cupboard, a tightly fitted lid of aluminium foil will suffice.

Bung in the oven and leave well alone for at least 2½ hours. Put your toes up and have a glass or two to give you strength to carry the dish to the table.

Half an hour before you are due to serve, take a peep and see if you need more stock, most of which will have been absorbed by the barley. Don't add too much extra stock as some of the joy of this dish is the thick gooey gravy-type liquid. Potatoes should have browned quite well.

Take to the table with lid still on, and remove with a flourish and roll of drums. Emanating smell is comforting and delicious. Serve with one boring vegetable such as leeks and one more colourful vegetable such as carrots, finished with butter and fennel seeds; or oven roasted peppers, asparagus or beetroot.

Chicken Safrina
Flora Hesketh

This is a perfect dish to give to unreliable guests. It is meant to take an hour and a half but it will not go hideously wrong if left for too long in the oven. This is a suitable recipe as Flora has the best chicken legs in London.

6 chicken thighs
1 box of baby tomatoes
2 courgettes
3 cloves of garlic
Bag of new potatoes

Brown off the chicken thighs in a pan. Slice the potatoes, tomatoes and courgettes. Lay them all mixed together, with the garlic in a casserole dish. Place the browned chicken on top and pop in preheated oven.

Diced Shoulder of Lamb in Parsley Pesto
Isobel Wood

The finest lamb in Britain comes from Isobel's company, Somerset Farm Direct. Isobel rears her own lambs in Somerset which are all slaughtered and sold directly from the farm. You can order your lamb and it is delivered directly to your home – if you wish you can even log on and see your lamb from birth and watch it grow before it is slaughtered and then eat it. The lambs are all allowed to roam the Somerset hills and have the happiest of lives, which ensures that eating them is always the happiest of experiences.

1 pack diced shoulder lamb (about 500g or 1lb)
1 large onion, chopped
Olive oil
150ml red wine
1 tbsp flour

For the pesto:
50g walnuts
Big bunch of parsley
25g parmesan
6 tbsp extra virgin olive oil

Sauté onions in two tbsp olive oil. Brown the meat and then add the flour, red wine and seasoning. Cook at 325°F / 170°C / Aga baking oven for two hours.

Meanwhile, make the pesto by mixing all of the pesto ingredients in a blender.

When the lamb is cooked, remove from the oven stir in parsley pesto and serve with creamy mashed potatoes.

Bobotie
Lucia Van der Post

I was born in South Africa and grew up in Cape Town at a time when there wasn't much *haute cuisine* around (these days it has restaurants that can hold their heads up with almost any in the world). Cape Town, you will remember, was established as a halfway house between Europe and the Far East, to provide the Dutch East Company employees with food and vitamins on their long journeys to the Dutch East Indies, from where the Dutch acquired not only their wealth but also a taste for spices.

Food at the Cape was heavily influenced by these oriental journeys and by Malaysian and Indonesian cuisine. My childhood memories of high days and holidays are of richly aromatic dishes, the mere thought of which can bring a tear to my eye to this day. This is not refined and elegant food – it is comfort food. However, it is interesting to note that when I served an array of Cape Malay dishes at my father's 80th birthday in London, to which event came highly sophisticated palates from around the world, the dishes (cold curried fish, bobotie and a meat fruit curry) were greeted with much delight. Bobotie could be said to be South Africa's national dish. Here is the version I served at my father's 80th birthday. It should be served with yellow rice – in South Africa they have a habit of adding raisins but personally I find them an abomination and I serve saffron rice gently spiced with cardamom, coriander and turmeric – and some cold salads.

1 thick slice white bread, broken into small bits
1 cup milk
2 tablespoons butter
2lbs ground lean lamb
1½ cups finely chopped onions
2 tablespoons Madras curry powder
1 tablespoon light brown sugar
¼ cup strained fresh lemon juice

(continued...)

3 eggs
1 medium-sized cooking apple, peeled, cored and finely grated
½ cup seedless raisins
¼ cup blanched almonds, coarsely chopped
4 small fresh lemon or orange leaves – if you can't get hold of them use 4 small bay leaves

Preheat the oven to 160°C.

Combine the bread and milk in a small bowl and let the bread soak for at least ten minutes.

Meanwhile, in a heavy pan 10" to 12" sauté pan, melt the butter over moderate heat. When the foam begins to subside, add the lamb and cook it, stirring constantly. Break up any lumps until the meat separates into granules and no traces of pink remain. Transfer the lamb to a deep bowl.

Pour off and discard all but two tablespoons of fat from the pan and drop in the onions, stirring frequently until they are soft and translucent but not brown. Add the curry powder, sugar, salt and pepper, and stir for one or two minutes. Add lemon juice and bring to a boil over high heat. Pour the entire mixture into the bowl of lamb.

Drain the bread in a sieve set over a bowl and squeeze the bread completely dry. Reserve the drained milk. Add the bread, one of the eggs, the apples, raisins and almonds to the lamb. Knead vigorously with both hands or beat with a wooden spoon until the ingredients are well combined. Taste for seasoning and add more salt if desired. Pack the lamb mixture loosely into a three-quart souffle dish. Tuck in the lemon, orange or bay leaves.

Beat the remaining two eggs with the reserved milk for about one minute or until they are well combined and begin to froth. Slowly pour the mixture evenly over the meat and bake in the middle of the oven for 30 minutes or until the surface becomes brown and firm to the touch.

Ferga's Burgers
Ferga O'Neill

Serves four

500g minced beef
250g minced lamb or pork
6 pickled gherkins, diced
1 small onion, diced
1 tbs Mixed herbs
1 and a half tbs tomato puree
Seasoning
Tabasco or 1 chilli
1 tbs Worcestershire sauce
1 egg
1 cup of grated medium Cheddar
1 ball of Mozzarella, diced

Combine all the ingredients in a bowl except for the cheeses, which you should mix together separately and divide into four portions. Make eight small balls from the mixture and flatten slightly (you will need two for each burger).
Take one ball and make a hollow in the centre and fill with one of the portions of cheese.
Take another ball and place on top of the cheese filled ball and mould together at the edges. Flatten into a burger shape.

Repeat for the other three burgers.

Barbecue or grill and serve with fresh tomato and lettuce on a bun.

Mrs Guard's Chicken
Rose Astor

Serves four

Learnt from my friend Ted's mother Mrs Guard who taught me
how to cook easy things that look impressive!

4 skinless chicken breasts (chicken supreme)
2 large flat Portobello mushrooms
500ml crème fraiche
2 tbsp white wine sherry
1 tbsp Dijon mustard
Salt and pepper

Put the chicken breasts and mushrooms (sliced) in an ovenproof
dish.
Mix the crème fraiche, mustard and sherry in a bowl and pour
over the chicken.
Put in the oven at 200°C for 45 minutes.

Beef Stew with Red Peppers and Olives
Lucy Hawkins

Serves 6

1kg organic beef, diced
30g seasoned plain flour
Olive oil
3 cloves garlic, sliced
2 medium onions, sliced in large chunks
1 can Guinness
350ml beef stock
1 bouquet garni
1 tbsp Dijon Mustard
1 dessert spoon brown sugar
6 green olives, quartered
2 red peppers, chopped

Cover the beef in the seasoned flour, until evenly coated.
Heat 1 tbsp olive oil in a frying pan.
Then brown the beef in small quantities and remove from the pan, adding extra oil as needed.
Fry the garlic in the same pan with any leftover flour for a few minutes.
Add the onions to the pan, cook for a few minutes to soften. Add the meat back into the pan with all of the following ingredients:
Guinness
Beef Stock
Bouquet Garni
Dijon mustard
Sugar
Bring the mixture up to a gentle simmer and then transfer to a pre-heated casserole dish.
Cook at 140°C for two and a quarter hours, adding the olives after one and a half hours and the red peppers after two, checking that the stew does not dry out – add more stock if needed.

French Partridge
Lord Fairhaven

An excellent way of serving a rather dull bird!

1 red legged partridge
1 shallot
1 clove garlic
1 fl oz calvados
4 fl oz white wine
2 tablespoons double cream

Brown the partridge in butter.
Add chopped shallot and garlic and cook for a few moments, deglaze with calvados and white wine.
Cover and cook for approximately twenty minutes.

Remove partridge.
Reduce sauce if necessary before adding cream.
Bring to the boil and pour over partridge.

Red Pesto Chicken
Olivia Stirling

For six to eight people

10 (organic) skinless chicken breasts
Olive oil
Salt and pepper
Two large tubes crème fraiche
1 pot red pesto sauce
Torn basil leaves
Cut chicken breast into finger thick strips using scissors

Into a large and heavy (Le Creuset) cooking pot, put a couple of good slugs of olive oil, salt and pepper. Fry the chicken strips over a gentle heat, turning often, until cooked through, but not necessarily browned, about 10 minutes. Add the crème fraiche, half the pot of red pesto and stir thoroughly, bringing to simmering point. Don't allow to bubble.

Adjust seasoning and add more pesto if required. Scatter basil leaves to add colour.

Dish up with brown rice and salad.

Poached Chicken Breasts in Whisky Sauce
Archbishop Conti

The archbishop married Henry and me in our family church on the side of a mountain. It is where all the Frasers are buried and one day I hope to be popped into the ground there in a groaning coffin.

2oz butter
2oz sliced leeks
2oz sliced carrots
2oz sliced onions
2oz sliced celery
1pt chicken stock
4 chicken breasts
2oz whisky, more if stronger flavour required
7oz crème fraiche
1 small teaspoon creamed horseradish
1-2 teaspoons honey warmed.

Melt butter in saucepan sauté leeks carrots onions and celery for three minutes. Add half the chicken stock and simmer for eight mins. Transfer to oven dish large enough to take the chicken breasts in one layer which are placed on top of the vegetables and the remaining stock poured over. Cover and cook in a medium oven until the chicken is tender.

Whisky Sauce:
In a saucepan heat the whisky, strain the chicken stock from the oven dish into the whisky and boil for three minutes. Draw the pan off the heat, add crème fraiche, horseradish, warmed honey, pepper and salt to taste, reheat and pour sauce over chicken in serving dish.

To give the dish a Scottish touch, it can be served with half a beef steak tomato stuffed with cooked haggis then baked in the oven covered with foil.

Pirozhki
Natalia Illingworth

Best bought puff pastry
Best quality finely ground beef
Onions (finely chopped and sweated in half butter and half oil
until golden and soft)
Salt and pepper
Tomato concentrate and Lea and Perrins (to taste)
Cumin and Red Pepper

Cook the onions, add the ground meat and other ingredients and
cook right through. Everything should be a little wet and VERY
tasty (not bland) so add the herbs and what you like to make it
all taste.

Roll out the pastry thinly.
Take a cup and press out round shapes (this should not be too thick
or so thin that when cooked the meat inside will burst but you do
not want them too thick so that one is only eating pastry!)
Place a spoonful of the cooked above meat mixture in the middle
of the round of pastry.
Brush the edges of the round with yolk of egg with a brush.
Pinch the edges together to make a half moon shape and ensure
all the edges are stuck together and that the meat is not going to
burst out when cooked.
Press the half moon shape you now have gently on the board so
that the base of it sits up right.

Brush the circular part of the pirozhki again with yolk of egg.
Place in oven for longer than you think, top shelf quite high until
golden brown.

When you eat these, the mixture should not be dry but tasty, juicy
and meaty.

Beef Stroganoff
Natalia Illingworth

Fillet or ribeye of beef
Onions (Spanish are best)
Mushrooms (lots)
Double cream
Tomato ketchup
Salt and pepper
Lea and Perrins
Butter
Sour cream if you can get it

Fry ordinary onions (sliced) in half butter and half good olive oil. If no olive oil, use all butter. Until golden brown, not burnt. Put into the dish you will serve the whole dish from (oven proof preferably).

Fry the sliced mushrooms lightly in sizzling butter but do not let go soggy. Should be al dente. Put into the dish above with the onions.

Cut up the fillet of beef or ribeye (excellent and cheaper) into finger size slices any old how or large dice cubes (fingers are easier). Fry these lightly all over in butter and a touch more but ensure you are not cooking the meat right through. When you think they are lovely, put into the dish above.

Pour the cream and rest of ingredients to taste all over the strog and stir all together and put in the oven to gently heat up (low gas or electricity). You must not let the whole thing over sizzle or bubble. If you do, the strog will be ruined.

Bon appetit.

Reliable Roast Chicken
Rita Konig

We rented Rita's flat while I was pregnant, it was a sanctuary of calm throughout, and I will never forget how delicious it always smelled when you opened the front door.

Shove half an onion and a lemon up the chicken's bottom with a bunch of thyme and some garlic.

Rub the outside with some olive oil, garlic, salt and pepper.

Slice a leek long ways and put in bottom of roasting tray. Lay the chicken upside down on the leeks. Add the other half of the onion to the roasting tray.

Put in the oven for about an hour to an hour and a half.

Check periodically, it may be an idea to pour some water in the tray if it is looking too dry.

Use the leeks and the onion to make the gravy by adding vegetable water and some wine. Do not go anywhere near it with cornflour.

You can add the leeks to the plate of vegetables as they are really delicious.

Roasted new potatoes:
Put new potatoes in a baking tray with some olive oil, rosemary and cloves of garlic.

Put in hot oven for forty minutes.

Utterly delish.

Smoked Pheasant Dish
Cecilia McEwan

We always smoke our pheasants, although smoked chicken would do. Cut the breasts thin, and place in neat lines in an oven proof dish.

Take enough cream to cover the breasts.

Mix in home-made chutney, cut fine on a plate or a good bought one. Add powdered mace, cumin and coriander, some Worcestershire sauce, a little curry paste, not too much. Cover the pheasant with foil and heat until ready. This is not a curry, but a spiced dish. Serve with rice.

Summer Chicken
Susannah Stourton

Our babies were due a day apart and so Suze and I have shared an extraordinary and magical journey together. Henry thinks that she is like a second husband to me.

4 large chicken breasts preferably organic / free range
½ jar of sun-dried tomatoes
1 packet of Parma ham
3 handfuls of pine nuts
3 tablespoon of chopped basil leaves

For dressing:
Balsamic vinegar
Olive oil
Mustard
Squeeze of lemon juice

Place the chicken breasts in the oven at 190°C for twenty minutes.
Remove and leave to cool.
Cut the chicken into 1 inch strips, place in a dish.
Cut up the sun-dried tomatoes and scatter over the chicken strips.
Cut the parma ham into medium sized pieces and scatter over chicken and sun-dried tomatoes.
Lightly toast the pine nuts and scatter them over the chicken dish
Make the dressing: 1 part vinegar, 2 parts olive oil, ½ teaspoon mustard, squeeze of lemon juice.

Pour the dressing over, ensure all the chicken has been dressed, and then sprinkle over the basil.

Roya's Seriously Simple Stir Fry
Roya Nikkah

Serves 4

4 chicken breasts or thin steaks
2 courgettes
2 carrots
1 white / Chinese cabbage
Oyster mushrooms
1 bunch of spring onions
1 stem of fresh ginger
1 clove of garlic
1 red/green chilli
1 lime
Sesame oil / soy sauce

Slice the chicken breast / steak and marinate in a bowl with a few splashes of soy sauce, the lime juice, a little finely chopped ginger and finely chopped chilli, salt and pepper.
Whilst the meat is marinating (leave for up to an hour) chop the vegetables, carrots, courgettes into thin stir fry slices.

Heat some sesame oil in a wok and add the rest of ginger, chilli and finely chopped garlic.

Put spring onions, carrots and cabbage into wok first and keep tossing, then add courgettes and mushrooms. Before vegetables are fully cooked, heat some sesame oil in a separate pan and cook meat until just browned. Do not put all of the marinade into the pan or the meat will stew instead of fry.

When meat is just brown, add it to the wok and stir in with vegetables for a further few minutes

Serve with rice or noodles!

Irish Stew
John and Helen Bond, The Plough, East Sheen.

After many years tending to the demands of thirsty Sloanes in The Duke of Wellington, Belgravia (see Roasted Pumpkin and Onion Soup), John and Helen have moved to The Plough in East Sheen, where I wish them all the luck in the world.

Before they set off on their new adventure, Helen was kind enough to give me this delicious recipe for her Irish Stews which I have enjoyed on many occasions.

Serves 4-6

2lb diced lamb
1 tablespoon flour
1 teaspoon salt
1 teaspoon paprika
Freshly ground pepper
2oz oil
2 onions peeled and sliced
1 clove garlic chopped
1 large carrot chopped
2-3 sticks celery
1pt water
1 heaped teaspoon caraway seeds
1 medium head green cabbage
4-6 potatoes peeled and diced
4 carrots, thickly sliced

Toss the meat in seasoned flour, fry off in oil. Remove.

Gently fry the onions, garlic, celery and carrots. Return meat to pan. Add stock and caraway seeds, bring to boil, cover and place in preheated oven (gas mk. 4/ 350°F/ 180°C) for 1¾ hours.

(continued...)

Cut cabbage into wedges, add cabbage, diced potato and sliced carrots to pot and extra water if necessary. Adjust seasoning. Cover and continue to cook for a further three quarters of an hour

Sprinkle with chopped parsley before serving.

Irish Stew

Piers' Hamburgers
Piers von Westenholz

I love spending time in this kitchen, it is full of wonderful paintings, old and new. Even the paint-by-numbers horse adds to the charm. Betty the dog dotes by the baron's feet as he cooks these excellent burgers and I chat to Fritz and Lofty over a bottle of wine. Heaven.

Rump steak
Fresh Herbs – lovage, chives, flat leaf parsley (lots)
Tomato ketchup
One egg yolk (organic)

Take ALL the fat off the meat, and cut into chunks.

Put all the above with salt and pepper to taste into a magimix and whiz for a few seconds, or until roughly chopped (do not overdo this).

Remove and mould into bun shapes, and place them into hot olive oil for as long as you want, depending on how well done you like the meat. As the ingredients are so fresh as little time as possible is perfect, then its like a warm steak tartare!

Persian Chicken
Mrs Raoul Lempriere Robin

Roast chicken
3 cups rice
5 cloves
¼lb blanched almonds
3 chopped chillies
Breadcrumbs
2 teaspoon lime or lemon juice
1 cup sour cream
¼lb of grapes
Grated cheese
2 oz raisins
½ tin sweetcorn
1 tin of asparagus tips
3 egg yolks
4 oz butter
2 bay leaves

Cook rice in 6 cups of water and cloves.

Strip meat off chicken in fifteen pieces. Stone grapes and raisins mix with rice, almonds, grapes asparagus, egg yolks, chills, cream lemon juice salt and pepper. Put in fire proof dish, cover with breadcrumbs and grated cheese. Cover with butter and bake. If too dry moisten with wine.

Pot Roast Haunch of Venison
Jimmy MacNab

Jimmy is a true Scotsman, never dressed in anything but his kilt. I had great difficulty getting this recipe as each time I spoke to Jimmy I could hardly hear a word above the sound of his hens, with whom he shares a house. The hens are washed and then blown dry by Jimmy in time for showing them at fêtes, he is devoted to them all. Jimmy will never have heard of a celebrity chef and eats recipes that will have been unchanged for the last 100 years like this one.

2 onions
3 carrots
2 parsnips
2 turnips
1 head celery
2 apples
5kg venison
cloves
8 fl oz olive oil
4 oz brown sugar
Dried mixed herbs
Fresh thyme, rosemary and mint
1½ bottles red wine

Finely chop the vegetables and apples place in the bowl of a large pot and set the haunch on top. Make several incisions in the top of the meat, inserting cloves as you go. Rub the olive oil and sugar into the meat, sprinkle over some dried mixed herbs and then some fresh thyme, rosemary and mint. Pour the wine into the pot and leave to marinate in a cool place for four days, turning occasionally.

When ready to cook, cover the pot with foil and place in the oven at 350°F. Allow twenty minutes for each pound of meat.

Oxtail
Patrick Lichfield

This, apparently, was one of Roald Dahl's favourites. It is one of mine too. When it was banned during the BSE crisis, I used to have friendly butchers who would kindly pass it under the counter to me surreptitiously.

2 oxtails fat trimmed off
4 tbls olive oil
3 medium onions finely chopped
3 carrots chopped
2 tbls flour
2 cloves garlic
2 tbls redcurrant jelly
2 pts strong beef or vegetable stock

Heat oil in a heavy casserole, brown oxtail all over. Set oxtail aside, lower heat and sauté onions and garlic until transparent, add carrots, stir, then put back oxtail cover with stock and lid. Place into oven 120°C for three hours. Lift out the oxtail with a slatted spoon onto dish, cover with foil and leave overnight with the stock covered in the casserole in fridge. The next day skim all the fat off the stock, placing some into a saucepan, over a moderate heat blend into the flour, stirring to make a roux. Take off the heat and add the jellied stock, put back on the heat and bring up to boil stirring continuously then simmer for 2-3 minutes, add the redcurrant jelly, continue to stir till dissolved.

Put oxtails into the sauce, place into oven 350°F for approx 1½-2 hours until cooked.

MAIN COURSE
(FISH)

Fish Pie
Leo Fenwick

My favourite recipe is fish pie, which I have always had a love for since I was child.

Put the fish fillets in an oven proof dish in a pre-heated moderate heat (190°C). The fillets can be haddock, cod or any white fish. Add to this braised scallops or fresh prawns, sautéed bacon pieces, shallots, chopped spring onion, chopped peeled and de-seeded tomatoes, hard boiled eggs or halved shell quail eggs and chopped parsley.

Bake the white fish for twenty minutes until just cooked. Take away the skin and any bones and place in a bowl. Melt a tablespoon of butter slowly over a low heat. Add a tablespoon of plain flour gradually and keep stirring and cooking it. Add salt and freshly ground pepper to taste. Slowly add the liquid. This should be a combination of fish stock (from supermarket or make your own from fish bones) and milk. This will swell the flour and butter. If you then add the liquid slowly the paste will become a smooth cream. Keep the heat on low but enough to cook the mixture as you stir it. Add Tomato Ketchup and anchovy sauce (Geo Watkins) to the bechamel sauce and stir. Pour the sauce over the chosen fish combination. Put into individual pie dishes or one large one. Peel and boil enough potatoes to cover the top of the quantity of fish pie mixture.

When boiled potatoes are soft, mash by hand to remove all lumps, then mix in some butter and the yolk of an egg, cream, crème fraiche or plain yoghurt (according to taste) and whisk (do not use magimix as this will turn it into potato glue!) Spread the mash over the top of individual or large bowls of fish mixture.

Decorate the top with a fork and store in the fridge until you need the dish or place directly in a hot oven or grill to brown the top.

Fish Baked in Salt
Fiona Allen

1 fish per person, or a large fish of about 1 kg, any firm, white fleshed fish, like seabass, will do. The fish must be whole, and must be absolutely fresh.
1 kg of coarse cooking salt.

Have the fish cleaned but not scaled (this is important or the salt will penetrate the skin and make the fish too salty).

Take an oven dish which will fit the fish, and pour in about a third of the salt. Put the fish in, and cover with the rest of the salt. The fish must be well covered all over with a thick layer.

Put this into a hot oven 210°C for 30-50 minutes, depending on the size of the fish. When you can smell fish, it is ready.

The salt will have solidified into a crust, break this and carefully remove the fish to a clean warm plate. Most of the skin will come off with the crust, but take off any left, and be careful to remove all the salt.

Serve with boiled potatoes and a green vegetable, and any sauce you like, or just a lemon to squeeze over it.

All the flavour is kept in by the salt and the fish tastes delicious.

Easy and Delicious Salmon
Mary Fellowes

Marinade fillets in 1 cm deep of light soy sauce, strips of ginger, fresh lime juice and chopped red chilli (de-seeded) and lots of black pepper, leave in fridge for 2 to 3 hours.

When ready to eat, either sear them with all the juices in a frying pan or place under the grill for 7-10 minutes. Serve with grated lime zest on fillet and also with a salad of sweet potato, spinach, rocket, walnuts, red onion and broccoli.

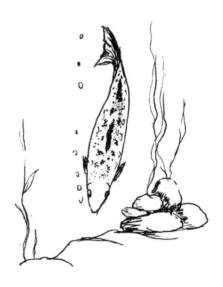

Vietnamese Summer Rolls with Nuoc Cham Dipping Sauce
Tom Lichfield

I ate so many of these during my years with Tom, I nearly turned into one.

The idea of this recipe is to make it up as you go along, add or get rid of any of the ingredients as you please.

My view on the Vermicelli noodles is, why waste valuable roll space with something that tastes of nothing!? So I leave them out!
Pork may also be added to replace the chicken and if you don't like coriander or bean sprouts....get rid of them!

Make the rolls as thin or fat as you like. The choice of filling is up to you.

These two are my favourites:

A handful of baby spinach leaves
8-12 sheets of rice paper (available from any oriental shop)
A bunch of fresh mint
A bunch of fresh coriander
A bunch of fresh Thai basil
2-3 free range chicken breasts – poached in chicken stock then diced / minced but not fine...
1-2 handfuls of cooked prawns – diced but not too fine
Half a packet of cooked and cooled Vermicelli noodles
A few spring onions – sliced lengthways into halves then quarters
Half a cucumber – seeds scraped out with a teaspoon & sliced lengthways finely
Half a carrot – slice lengthways very finely
A big handful of bean sprouts

Fill a large bowl with boiling water and dip each rice paper sheet into them for fifteen seconds (or until they become soft). Take them out and lay them on damp cloths to cool down.

(continued...)

Once cool, place a row of spinach leaves down the centre, then a row of Mint, basil, and coriander leaves (try to cover at least half the rice paper with the herbs and spinach to act as a protective layer).

Add a layer of prawn, chicken or both.

Add a sprinkle of bean sprouts a few strips of carrot, cucumber, and spring onion.

Another layer of spinach on top like a blanket.

Roll as best you can tightly, once forwards. Then push the sides in and fold any excess rice paper into the middle, and roll forwards (away from you) as tightly as possible without tearing the roll. Practice makes perfect!

They should be cut in the centre at a slight diagonal, served at room temperature and dipped in the dipping sauce below.

Nuoc Cham:

This is a traditional Vietnamese dip and my favourite. It is a bit like a milder fish sauce. Some people prefer sweet chilli sauce, or hoi sin sauce which both work well, both are available from most supermarkets.

Mince 6 garlic cloves
Finely chop 3 red chillies (seeds removed for less spicy)
A nob of grated ginger (small one)
A lime
100ml of water
50ml of rice vinegar
50ml of Thai fish sauce
50 g of caster sugar

(...continued overleaf)

(continued from previous page...)

Put the above ingredients into a saucepan and warm without boiling.

Let the sugar dissolve and the flavours combine.

Take of the heat and leave to cool.

Once cool, add the juice of the lime and serve.

(A dribble of sesame oil tastes very good too)

Lemon Grass dip :

Do exactly as above, but also bash, bruise, and finely chop two sticks of lemon grass.

Add to the mixture before heating.

Once the flavours are combined, take off the heat, put it in the fridge for minimum of three hours.

Stir in the lime before serving (at room temp).

Again, these flavours can be increased or decreased according to personal taste.

Grandma Rigg's Indian Kedgeree
Rachael Stirling and Diana Rigg

Stationed in Jodhpur with my grandfather in the 1930s and 1940s, the tinned and dry ingredients of this seriously comforting dish proved a practical store cupboard stand by for my grandmother Beryl, and is fondly remembered by my own mother. It has been a favourite Sunday night supper dish of mine for as long as I can remember.

300g Basmati rice – cooked and well drained
2 tins sardines in olive oil
2 hard boiled eggs
Handful of sultanas
Flaked almonds – a tablespoonful
Large onion, sliced

Mash sardines and oil from tin in serving dish. Add rice, well drained. Mix together with sultanas. Fry onion until sweet and brown, spread on top of rice, grill almonds until brown (watch these as they burn the minute you look away) and scatter on top, together with hard boiled egg chopped. Cover dish with tin foil and place in oven at 180°C for twenty minutes.

Serve with green salad and Sharwoods hot Bengal chutney.

Pesce Spada al Forno
Anna Maria Constable Maxwell

4 fillets of swordfish
4 lemons
150g breadcrumbs
1 teaspoon of oregano
1 teaspoon of chopped parsley
Chilli
Olive oil

Marinade in a bowl for thirty minutes the fish with olive oil, lemon juice, grated lemon peel, oregano, salt and a pinch of chilli.
Then press the fish slices into a mixture of breadcrumbs and parsley and place into a greased roasting pan. Sprinkle a little bit of oil on them. Put into a hot oven for thirty minutes. Serve garnished with slices of lemon.

Vongole

Light Chilli Prawn Lunch
Erskine Berry

I've known Ersk since we both used to eat mud pies together as babies up the glen in Scotland.

Thick bottomed frying pan
Olive oil
1 red onion
1 clove garlic
1 large red chilli pepper
1 tblsp fresh coriander
2 tblsp tomato paste and tinned tomatoes if needed to supplement the sauce
25/30 tiger prawns
Splash white wine

Chop the onion, garlic and soften in oil. Add the chopped chilli till it's cooking and then the tomato paste. The mixture will thicken and add the wine till its all absorbed and starting to simmer. At that point bring on the prawns with the coriander following shortly and gently stir until all cooked.

Serve with mash potato made with olive oil and crème fraiche (not butter) and baby spinach salad.

Tuna with Salsa
Alice Lutyens

Serves two

2 tuna loin steaks
1 pack fresh basil
Half pack flat leaf parsley
1 tblsp capers
4 anchovy fillets (depending on taste – I often have more)
1 small lemon
1 shallot
1 clove garlic
4 tblsp virgin olive oil

Tear the basil and parsley.

Grind the garlic, capers, anchovies and shallot together with a pestle and mortar.

Mix all ingredients together in a bowl (excluding the tuna). Gently warm them over a very low heat – you don't want them to even simmer, just warm up a bit.
Cook the tuna steaks over the heat, preferably on a griddle pan, but frying pan will do. It will take approx two or three minutes on each side if you wish them to be medium rare.
Place the tuna on a warmed plate, and spoon the salsa over the top. Add a drizzle of extra virgin olive oil over the top – you don't want it to be dry.

Please note that this recipe is a guideline only – some prefer more or less of the anchovies and capers. It is possible to leave one out entirely.

Pickled Herrings
Jimmy MacNab

This recipe is meant to be prepared so far in advance that in our modern culture it seems beyond imagination to even think of doing such a thing, which is rather why I love this recipe.

This is delicious served with brown bread and butter. Salting was the traditional way of preserving herrings when they were plentiful. Be sure to start these at least eleven days ahead.

4lb salt herrings
3 large onions
1 tablespoon mixed herbs
1 tablespoon rosemary
1 tablespoon sweet paprika
1 tablespoon crushed chillies
Dill
Black and white peppercorns
6-8 cloves
3 tablespoons allspice
2 pints good quality malt vinegar
1¼lb dark brown sugar

Cut the herrings in half, taking out the back fin as you go. Soak the fish in cold water for at least 36 hours.
Chop the herrings into 1 inch pieces and mix well with the chopped onions. Next mix in all the other ingredients except for the vinegar and sugar and leave for three hours.
Boil the vinegar and sugar in a pan until the sugar has dissolved completely. Place the herring mixture into sterilized pickling jars and pour over the sweetened vinegar. Leave for four days, turning each jar upside down once daily to ensure that the vinegar penetrates all the fish. The herrings can be eaten after four days, but improve in flavour if left for longer.

Archie's Asian-Style Spicy Seared Tuna Salad
Archie Keswick

This is a very versatile, fresh, light, crunchy salad with a good Asian kick to it. Easily adaptable with any fresh in-season veg or meat.

For 4 people

4-8 carrots (cleaned, peel off the skin and discard, then continue peeling the remainder into long strings / julienned)
1 box of cherry toms or a handful vine toms (cleaned and quartered)
5 stalks of celery (cleaned and chopped very finely to make thin U-shaped bites)
5 shallots (purple or banana; chopped finely)
$\frac{1}{4}$-$\frac{1}{2}$ of cucumber (halved lengthways and finely sliced to create half-moon shaped pieces)
Mint leaves & Coriander leaves (good bunch, torn or shredded)
1 bunch Spring Onions (finely chopped)
2 large raw tuna steaks
optional extras / equivalents (in any amount): Beansprouts, vermicelli rice noodles (soaked) cashew nuts, cress, mung beans, raw French beans, dried shrimp (a tablespoon max), peanuts.
cooked chicken breast, sliced pork neck fillet or sliced rare steak (delicious!!), peppers, mushrooms... not lettuce leaves though.

Asian Dressing:
2-4 coriander roots (a couple of coriander stems chopped very finely will suffice)
2 cloves of garlic
1-3 small birds eye chillies (careful when chopping as incredibly spicy!!)
$\frac{1}{2}$ teaspoon of whole black peppercorns.
2 tbl spoons fish sauce
1-2 lemons
1tsp brown sugar or palm sugar

(continued...)

Put coriander root, chillies, peppercorns and garlic into a pestle and mortar and bang until a paste (can be pasted gently in a normal bowl with the end of a rolling pin), then add the juice of 1 lemon (minus pips), 2 tbsp of fish sauce and the sugar. Keep mixing and tasting as you go along. If it is too fishy add more lemon, if too lemony, then add fish sauce.

In a large salad bowl add all the salad ingredients together.
On a medium heat, lightly oil a griddle pan (with sunflower, peanut or corn oil, not olive). Sear each side of the tuna steak for 1 or 2 mins max turning only once. The more you fiddle with the steaks while they're cooking the more likely they are to break up. The idea is to cook the outside leaving middle near raw.
Remove seared tuna. Place on a chopping board and roughly chop bite-sized chunks.
Now all that needs to be done is mix the salad and the warm tuna pieces together and garnish with ripped coriander and mint leaves and pour over generous amounts of the delicious spicy dressing.

Happy Scoffing!

mint.

Kianjibbi Kedgeree
Richard O'Hagan

For a hundred years now since the great days of coffee prospecting in Kenya began, the O'Hagan's of Kianjibbi Estate, Kiambu have celebrated the great tradition of Kedgeree for breakfast. On Sunday morning this wonderful tradition is accompanied by the chimes of 'Alleluia' as Handel's Messiah floats through the verandah to the dining room.

Kedgeree (and the Messiah) for eight.

4 hard boiled duck eggs
2lbs cooked smoked haddock
1lb boiled white rice

The juice of 1 lemon
½ pint of single cream 4 oz butter

Place the haddock in a shallow dish and poach with a little milk for about twenty minutes until nice and flaky in the oven.

Cut the duck eggs into wedges and blend with the flaked fish and rice.

Season to taste with salt, cayenne pepper and a little nutmeg. Stir in the cream and butter a deep dish.

Put the mix in the dish, dot the remaining butter on top,
Bake in the centre of pre-heated oven at 180°C for 30 minutes.

Garnish with chopped parsley, turn on the Messiah and serve!

Sebastian's Tuna
Sebastian Gibson

I have a sort of signature supper party dinner that I do as it looks fairly impressive and is not very hard work for someone like me who is not a great cook.

It is tuna steaks with an avocado salsa, cous cous and griddled courgette.

For the Salsa:
Dice a ripe avocado, red onion, plum tomato, coriander and basil. Mix this finely diced mixture (by hand) with a generous amount of good quality olive oil, a bit of lemon and some balsamic vinegar. Leave to marinate. Vary quantities according to how many people you are having.

Follow instructions on Sammy's Organic Cous Cous With Herbs (you can buy from Waitrose) and the cooking process involves pouring boiling water onto it.

Flash fry your tuna steaks in a griddle pan (I like them quite raw in the middle and think this works with the salsa), then add some more oil and crushed garlic to the pan and fry some finely sliced courgettes.

The whole process should take no more that thirty minutes and you can serve up each plate with a tuna steak, courgette and cous cous on it and let people help themselves to the salsa. The salsa really makes it so it's best to over-cater on that side and you can always use it the following day if you have left-overs.

Soothing Creamed Sweetcorn Chowder with Minced Chicken and Butterflied Prawns
Archie Keswick

2 cans of creamed sweetcorn (can be bought in Asian supermarkets, Sainsbury's or Waitrose)
1 bunch of spring onions (topped 'n' tailed and finely chopped)
10-20 raw prawns (preferably tiger but others will suffice, wash and de-vein by gently running a knife down the spine of the prawn allowing them to open up (butterfly) and give you access to the vein which is discarded. Frozen prawns often come de-veined already)
2-3 breasts of chicken (chopped finely, all similar sizes, approx 2cm sq pieces)
Chicken stock / bouillon (if in liquid form 1½ pints, if stock cubes 1-2 cubes)
Coriander bunch with roots intact if possible
5 cloves of garlic (finely chopped)
1 medium white onion (finely chopped)
1 tbsp brown sugar or palm sugar
1-3 bird's eye chillies (finely chopped)
Pepper and soy to garnish.

Finely chop garlic, onion and some coriander root (2 pieces) and fry in a lug of sunflower or peanut oil (not olive!) on a medium heat in a large soup pan or heavy-based casserole dish. I like to add a lug of Shaoxing Chinese rice wine at this point to give a unique flavour – dry sherry can be used as a replacement. Do allow the alcohol to burn off though.

Once nicely browned add either your stock or boiling water and your stock cubes and allow to gentle simmer for ten minutes. The dish should be ¾ full with liquid now.

(continued...)

Now add the cans of creamed sweetcorn and allow to heat up. Once this is on a gentle roll add your chicken to the soup and cook for approx two minutes (until it starts to turn noticeably white) before you add the raw prawns. The prawns once heated will curl extensively as desired.

Taste the soup to see how it is. If there is not enough flavour and seems bland, either add some Teryaki sauce (a tbsp), soy or more stock / bouillon.

When satisfied add lots of ground black pepper, a really good bunch of coriander leaves and serve very hot. Do make sure you don't faff around too much once you think the prawns are done as they (and the chicken) continue to cook in the finished product when the diners bowl is in front of them.

Hey presto...a deliciously, soothing, sweet, savoury, spicy corn chowder with butterfly prawns and chicken...yummy yum..!

MAIN COURSE
(PASTA)

Vincisgrassi
Blanche Vaughan

Blanche is a professional chef, having worked in the kitchens at Moro, The River Café, and St. John's. This 18th century recipe comes from the Walnut Tree. She first gave this to us when I took Henry to meet her at her home in Herefordshire. In the middle of the night, he was found in the fridge finishing the pan of truffle lasagna, and it remains his favourite place to stay to this day.

Serves 6
Pasta:
500g flour
2 whole eggs
4 yolks
Salt

Sauce:
400g porcini, sliced (you can use dry)
200g Parma ham, sliced
1.2 litres milk
100g flour
150g butter
200g single cream
60ml extra virgin olive oil
Chopped parsley, salt and pepper
Grated parmesan, truffle oil (or shaved white truffle)

Make the pasta dough by mixing together the ingredients then kneading well. Roll through a pasta machine as for lasagna and cut into sheets to fit your baking dish (approx 12cm square would suit this). Cook in plenty of boiling salted water, a few at a time, until soft and place on linen cloths to drain.

For the sauce melt 50g of the butter, add the flour and blend well.

(continued...)

Heat the milk and add a little at a time, beating well. Cook the porcini in the olive oil then add to the béchamel. Stir in parma ham, cream, parsley and season. Bring to the boil then turn off the heat.

To assemble: butter a gratin dish, cover the bottom with a layer of pasta. Dot with butter, sprinkle over parmesan. Continue this process making layer after layer, finishing with béchamel and a sprinkle of cheese.

Cook in an oven preheated to 220°C /425°F for 20 mins. Serve with truffle oil or better still fresh shaved white truffle and a sprinkle more parmesan.

porcini

Quick, Simple Tomato Sauce
Henry Deedes

Unless you can be bothered to germinate your own tomatoes in one of those grow-your-own bags at home, I suggest you give fresh toms a swerve since your sauce is unlikely to taste of anything, so use tinned ones. Ever since I started cooking, I've tried hundreds of variations of tomato sauce recipes none of which did much for me. I found this one in a weekend supplement recently and it is by far the best, if not a little unusual. So whoever came up with it, thanks.

1 tin of plum tomatoes
1 shallot, peeled
1 tsp sugar
1 sprig of rosemary
Butter

Purée the tomatoes until smooth and place in a pan with the peeled shallot, the rosemary, sugar and a nice knob of butter. Cover and simmer on a low heat for half an hour. Remove shallot and rosemary and finish with another knob of butter to silk it up a bit. Serve with fussilli pasta shapes (the twirly ones), French bread, and enjoy.

Rosemary

Kirkton's Gnocchi
Joanna Fraser

500g potato gnocchi
200g diced smoked bacon or lardons
200g cherry tomatoes
300ml crème fraiche
200g Philadelphia cream cheese
200g grated gruyere
1 bag of baby spinach
1 large onion
3 cloves of garlic
Parmesan

Soften onion and garlic in olive oil, add crème fraiche, Philadelphia, gruyere and season to taste.

Fry bacon separately and tomatoes for the last minute and add to above.

Wilt the spinach in a pan and spread over base of oven proof dish.

Bring gnocchi to boil, strain and place all over spinach.

Pour on your gooey mixture, cover in grated parmesan.

Bake for ten minutes in hot oven.

Good additions: basil, truffle oil, pine nuts.

Pasta con le Sarde
Anna Maria Constable Maxwell

500g bucatini
500g fresh sardines
250g wild fennel
3 tomatoes
3 anchovies fillets
1 clove of garlic
20g raisins
20g pine seeds
1 dash saffron
100g fresh breadcrumbs
Salt and pepper

Clean the fennel and boil in salted water, drain them and keep the water to cook the bucatini pasta in it. Clean the sardines taking off the heads and dorsal fins. Using a wide high-sided pan fry lightly the chopped garlic together with the anchovies. Add the raisins, pine seeds, a sprinkle of saffron, the sardines, black pepper and a good pinch of salt and fry everything.

In a separate pan, fry the fennel in a little olive oil. Add it to the sardines, add the chopped tomatoes and cook at a low temperature, stirring every so often to make the sauce well amalgamated. In the water of the fennel add some salt and cook the bucatini but leave it very al dente because they continue cooking in the oven. Before draining add a sprinkle of saffron. Drain and mix with two thirds of the sauce.

Put in to a greased pan and sprinkle with breadcrumbs and pour the remaining sauce over the pasta.

Put into a hot oven for about ten minutes to amalgamate the flavours.

Macaroni Cheese
Molly Stirling

I had to badger Molly for almost two years before I finally got this recipe, days before this book went to press. Her recipe has made the book for me as macaroni cheese is my most favourite supper.

Put a knob of butter in a hot pan and wait till it melts. Stir in some white flour until you have doughy ball, somewhere in between solid and liquid. Slowly add milk whilst stirring very fast – just bit by bit very slowly, or the sauce will go lumpy. Keep adding the milk (you can increase the amounts as it turns into a sauce). Wait until you have a liquid sauce, and then you can add the grated cheese. I use some Red Leicester, some medium Cheddar and a bit of parmesan. DON'T hold back on the cheese as an uncheesy cheese sauce is disgusting.

Keep stirring.

Once the cheese is melted the sauce should be thicker but still quite runny. If it is too thick it is like school macaroni cheese that doesn't move on your plate. Add lots of pepper and LOTS of Colman's English mustard and stir some more.

Boil some macaroni in a pan of salted water, according to instructions on the packet.

When cooked, mix the macaroni with the sauce (should be quite saucy and not at all dry) and put in an over-proof dish. Then sprinkle more cheese over the top. Place under a hottish grill until brown and crispy on the top.

Serve with a green salad and lots of ketchup.

Al's Chilli Cherry Tomato Spag Sauce
Alice Irwin

I spend a huge amount of weekends rushing down to stay with Al in Dorset heaven. Whilst balancing a job, new baby, husband and miscreant dog, she inevitably manages to rustle up something delicious in a haphazard manner and this is something I always make a request for. She has given up asking me to help in the kitchen after I ruined several of her dishes, and managed to make lumpy mashed potato using an electric masher.

2 birdeye chillies (one red, one green) both med in size, you can use more if you need more heat
1 tin of anchovies in their oil
Big chunky handfuls of fresh basil
5 cloves of garlic (less if you want to kiss a prince)
Cherry toms on the vine (go for ripe-ish looking ones) one pack, or fill brown paper bag
1 pack good spag
Lots of black pepper
A small amount of Maldon sea salt
Half a teaspoon of white sugar
Half a lemon

Get your pan of boiling water bubbling away (add little amount of oil and some crushed salt).
In separate pan add a good glug of olive oil and gently warm.
Chop up garlic and chillies (inc their seed) and infuse gently in the oil, don't let boil.
Chop up anchovies, tear half of the basil, and chop all toms in half.

Add all this to the infusing garlic and chilli oil.
Add copious amounts of back pepper and the salt.
Stir all together, don't let boil, but keep on a good heat.

(continued...)

Your spag should now be cooking.

Leave the sauce to cook away, you will notice the toms go soft and you get a mushy looking sauce.

When spag is ready mix in the sauces, add more black pepper, the rest of the basil and a quick squidge of the lemon, hey presto and gobble when hot.

Caponata
Anna Maria Constable Maxwell

4 aubergines
200g olives
50g capers
2 big bunches of celery
4 tomatoes
2 large onions, cut in fine slices
1 glass of vinegar
1 spoon of sugar
Basil
Olive oil

Cut the aubergines into cubes and put them into a bowl of salted water to soak for about two hours. Clean the celery and place into salted water for five minutes.

Put the capers into a bowl with hot water to take away the salt and drain them after a few minutes. In a big frying pan put the onion with a little olive oil together with the capers and the chopped olives.

Add four peeled ripe tomatoes after having removed the seeds and cut them into pieces. Mix with a wooden spoon. Turn off the heat when a dense sauce forms. Dry the aubergines and fry them in a separate frying pan.

Using the same oil, fry the chopped celery sticks. Put the aubergine and fried celery pieces in the frying pan with the sauce, mix well and allow the flavours to amalgamate for five minutes under a low flame.

Sprinkle with sugar, pour the vinegar and after a few minutes turn off the heat and cover the pan with a lid.

The caponata is best cold, served in a terracotta bowl and garnished with a sprig of basil.

Thai Prawn Spaghetti
Bee Rice

Bee's baby's monthly nurse said to her, 'Why do you keep on eating after you are full? Why do you have to keep on going until you are in pain?' Here's why.

For 4 people

4 medium sized mild chillies (I use a mixture of red and green but either would do)
3 cloves of garlic
A generous sized chunk of fresh ginger
1 lemon
1 lime
Parsley
Coriander

Small prawns – they should be cooked and peeled and preferably from cold water eg. N. Atlantic
350g/ 450g spaghetti (not quick cook) depending on how big the eaters are!

Finely chop garlic/ chilli/ ginger and fry it in a light olive oil for about 5 mins. Do not burn it.
Add generous amount of salt and pepper and leave to sit while you cook the pasta.
When the spaghetti is nearly ready, turn on the heat on the frying pan again and give the prawns a quick heat through (2 mins) then add the juice from the lemon and lime.
Drain the pasta (should be al dente) and splash some olive oil on it so it doesn't stick.
Stir in the sauce and prawns.
Lastly add a generous handful of coarsely chopped parsley and coriander.
Serve with a green salad.

Sausage Bolognese
Justin Spink

Justin is a visionary who transforms people gardens into magical kingdoms.

For four people

½ pound of Pat's best herby sausages*
2 cloves garlic crushed
1 large white onion diced
1 large red pepper diced
1 tin chopped tomatoes
1 jar pasta sauce (of your choice)
1 handful of fresh basil
1 handful of fresh flat leaf parsley
1 large glass of red wine
1 bag of fresh spaghetti
Season to taste

Use a large frying pan or wokever. Put about two table spoons of olive oil in pan and heat, then add the onion, garlic and red pepper. Fry this until soft.

Slice open the sausages and break up the meat in the pan, continue to fry the mixture until the meat starts to brown.

Now add the tomatoes and pasta sauce of your choice. Add the wine and stir well and season, then let the mixture simmer for about fifteen minutes stirring occasionally.

Add the herbs and heat through just before serving with the freshly cooked spaghetti.

*Available from Pat Thomas, Market Square, Faringdon, Oxon.

Spaghetti Sauce
Virginia Fraser

I once lived with Virginia on my gap year (until I flooded the house) and would squeal with joy when I returned home and found this waiting in the kitchen.

In a saucepan fry a chopped onion, a chopped carrot and two chopped (finely) rashers of bacon. When soft add half a chicken cube and three tablespoons of tomato concentrate. Simmer for two minutes. Add two tins of Italian peeled tomatoes and leave to simmer for half an hour stirring once or twice.

mousetrap.

Champion Pasta Sauce
Rose Davidson

Rose is a champion jockey and is incredibly tough and resilient and yet when not in the saddle dresses in the most feminine stylish manner. She says that this is the perfect supper after a day charging around on the horses.

2 red onions
7 sausages, spicy if preferred
1 tablespoon rosemary
2 bay leaves
2 chillies
2 tins tomatoes
Red wine
150ml double cream

Block of parmesan

Tablespoon of anchovy essence

Fry the onion in some olive oil. When slightly brown add the sausage meat which you have taken out of the sausage skins, herbs and chilli. Cook for twenty minutes on a lowish heat. Spoon off most of the fat leaving behind a spoon full. Poor in the wine and add the tomatoes. Leave for ten minutes to cook on a medium high heat.

Add to cooked pasta with the cream and generous helping of parmesan. Yum Yum.

Clammy Pasta
Laura Lopes

Laura lives for her dry white wine, cigarettes and shellfish. She is the only person I know who will eat a plate of oysters followed by a bowl of chopped shallots and red wine vinegar with almost as much enjoyment.

Ok now my delish recipe. I did it last night and Harry said it was my best.

Serves 2
16 small clams in shells
Angel hair pasta
12 cherry tomatoes
12 sun blushed tomatoes
4 cloves of garlic
2 small Thai chillies
Olive oil
Half a lemon

Halve the cherry toms and sprinkle with some olive oil and two cloves of garlic (whole and skinned) put in the oven (gas mark 5) until roasted and soft. Finely chop the chilli, two remaining cloves of garlic and roughly chop the sun dried toms.

Boil large pan of boiling water and cook pasta. At the same time get another saucepan gently fry the garlic and chilli and add the clams. Let them steam until open (4-5 mins) and squeeze the lemon juice. Let all the juices simmer gently in the saucepan.

When the pasta is ready, drain and add oil and pepper. Toss the roasted toms and sun blushed toms and add in the steaming clams.

Serve immediately.

ODDS AND ENDS

Vinaigrette
Drusilla Fraser

My mother is famed for this recipe which stems from an old French cook at her grandparents' house. I do have to admit though I have never been able to make it as well as hers despite watching her for the last 27 years, good luck.

1 heaped teaspoon of Dijon mustard
1 heaped teaspoon salt (I use Maldon sea salt)
2 heaped teaspoons of caster sugar
Lots and lots of pepper – freshly ground
1 big fat juicy garlic clove
1 tablespoon red wine vinegar
6 tablespoons of sunflower oil (or light oil)

Whisk madly together and add to a salad.

Caesar Salad Dressing
Tiffany Butterfield

2 eggs
2 tbsp grated parmesan
1 tbsp chopped garlic
1 tbsp Dijon mustard
1 tbsp Lea and Perrins
1 tsp lime juice
Salt and pepper

¼ cup white wine vinegar
1 ¼ cup oil (½ olive oil, ½ sunflower oil)
2 sliced anchovies

Whizz eggs in a magimix, add all other ingredients except vinegar and oil and whiz again for about ten seconds. Add vinegar, whiz until mixed properly. Then while the magimix is on, slowly add the oil until it is thoroughly mixed. It has to be quite runny so it doesn't matter if you add the oil too quickly.

Onion Gravy
Violet von Westenholz

4 large onions
Light or mild olive oil
½ pint stock
Plain flour (through a sieve)
2 spoons redcurrant jelly
Red wine

Slice up the onions and fry gently over a low heat until soft, be careful not to burn them. Remove from the heat, add the flour stirring thoroughly and slowly pour in the stock. Return to the heat and spoon in the redcurrant jelly to make a thickish sauce.

Lastly pour in the red wine and leave to simmer.

Big J's Chilli Oil
Johnny Hopkins

A beautiful bottle of chilli oil not only spices up your meal, but also the look of your kitchen and dinner table.

It is child's play to make and it can be customised according to your tolerance of hot food and preference of herbs and spices.

You need a CLEAR BOTTLE (glass) and some DRIED RED CHILLIES, that's it! Use a clear bottle because this will flaunt the lovely orange colour to all your buddies – *very* sexy! An empty white wine / rosé bottle is fine if you can't be bothered to buy one from a shop. You will need an oil drizzle top however, which are easy to find in any kitchen store (about £1).

Pour a handful of dried chillies into the empty bottle. Then simply fill it up with good quality extra virgin olive oil. The more chillies you use, the hotter it will be, so it's better to start small and aim high. Leave the mixture to fuse for 2-3 weeks until it turns that warm orange colour. Hey presto, that's it! It is particularly good with pasta dishes, but believe me, you'll become addicted.

To refill, just add more oil. EXPERIMENT!

Try combinations of your favourites: ginger, garlic, thyme, rosemary etc xxx

Spiced Ham Sauce
Venetia Lang

To 8 oz cooked ham allow:

1 oz butter
1 oz brown sugar
3 tablespoons vinegar
2 tablespoons redcurrant jelly (or cranberry jelly)
1 or 2 teaspoons mustard
Good scrunch of pepper.

Put all ingredients into a saucepan and heat gently until the jelly has melted.

Pour sauce over the ham and heat gently in the oven. Watercress is good with it.

Lentils
Leonora Grosvenor

*Apart from being a wonderful artist, Leonora is famed for her cooking.
I hope one day to be able to cook half as well and with the same level
of calm. One of my most favourite people.*

250g puy lentils
1½ red onions, finely chopped
3 thick slices of chorizo, cubed
2 cloves of garlic
1 teaspoon of dried or fresh thyme
1 tablespoon of sun-dried tomato paste
1 tablespoon balsamic vinegar
3 tablespoons roasted pine nuts
Chopped parsley
Chicken stock
Sea salt and pepper

Cook the lentils in the chicken stock with two cloves of garlic. Fry
onions in a little oil and butter until golden, add the chorizo and
cook a little longer. When lentils are cooked, add onions, chorizo,
pine nuts, tomato paste and vinegar. Stir well and remove garlic.

Keep warm and just before serving add the chopped parsley and
mix well and season. Delicious with roast lamb or sausages.

Lake Palace Aubergines
Katie Farquhar

Serves 6
1¾lb Aubergines
1" fresh ginger
3 large cloves garlic
2 oz water
1 tsp fennel seeds
½ tsp cumin seeds
1 tablespoon ground coriander
1/4 tsp tumeric
1 tin of organic chopped tomatoes
Oil and seasoning
Mozzarella cheese

Slice the aubergines, sprinkle with salt and leave in colander to drain. Pat dry, fry in oil or put on baking try in oven with oil. In blender, put water, garlic, ginger and whiz until fairly smooth. Heat three tablespoons of oil in pan and add fennel and cumin. Fry for one minute then add tomato mixture to tumeric. Cook for five more minutes. Arrange aubergines in oven proof dish, pour mixture on top, then mozzarella. Bake in oven for fifteen minutes.

Cauliflower Cheese
Ben Warrack

Ben could literally charm the midges from the hills.

Make a white sauce. If this seems daunting then consult one of the masters (Delia Smith has various techniques). If other cookery books leave you cold then the following routine usually works. Take a decent lump of butter (an ounce – or just under a quarter of a normal pat of the stuff) and melt it in a small saucepan. Then slowly add in about two tablespoons of flour (again about an ounce), stirring all the time. This should make a gloopy sort of molten lava mixture. Stir a lot on the heat for a couple of minutes allowing the flour to cook a bit. Take this off the heat and allow to cool for a minute. While off the heat stir in half to three-quarters of a pint of milk. Put back on the heat and stir continuously to avoid lumps (optimistic but it does happen sometimes). When properly hot add a couple of handfuls of grated cheese (any form of hard cheese goes nicely), salt and pepper.

While this has been going on boil some water and lightly cook the heads of a large cauliflower (or two small ones) for 3-4 minutes. Drain and put the cauliflower into a dish, add the cheese sauce (and some bits of fried bacon if you are feeling flash) and grate some extra cheese on top. Put in a medium to hot oven for 20-30 minutes.

Cauliflower cheese goes brilliantly with almost anything but is particularly good with sausages, lamb chops or cold ham.

Zucchine Frite
Christabel Lawson Johnston

Christabel is convinced that she wooed her husband by cooking him endless amounts of these.

Courgettes
Vegetable oil for deep frying
Salt
6oz chickpea flour
½ teaspoon baking powder
1 teaspoon cornflour
½ tablespoon each of ground cumin, coriander, mild curry powder and turmeric

Place all the batter ingredients in a large bowl, mix well then stir in enough water to form a light batter. Place all the vegetables in the batter, stir well and coat and leave for 30 minutes.
Heat the oil to 350°C. Drop tablespoons of the vegetables in batter one by one into the hot oil and fry until golden and crisp.

Drain on paper towels and season lightly with a little salt.

Sauté Fennel
Fiona Allen

As many fennel bulbs as necessary
Fennel seeds (if you really love the taste of fennel)
Salt and pepper
Olive oil

Cut the tough root of the bottom of the bulb, and the green tops. Discard the tough outer layer, and cut up the remaining bulb in thick slices.

Cover the bottom of a sauté pan with good olive oil and heat well. Add the fennel, salt, pepper and fennel seeds and cook on a high heat until the pieces are lightly browned. Lower the heat and cover with the lid, and cook until tender.

Very good with roast meats.

Ink cap mushrooms

Polish Potato Dumplings
Danuta Mazur

Danuta is the only person I would ever trust with my skin. She is the finest facialist in London and I make my pilgrimages to her as often as I can. She always has something delicious waiting for me in her kitchen and these are exceptionally good.

2lbs potatoes
4 eggs
2 tsp fresh parsley
3 tbs breadcrumbs
Butter

Cook potatoes in boiling, salted water. Drain and mash.

Combine with the egg yolks, parsley and breadcrumbs. Season to taste and then fold in stiffly beaten egg whites. Stir lightly. Divide into little dumplings. Drop by the spoonful into boiling water, cover and steam until dumplings rise to the top. Remove with a perforated spoon, drain and serve with a little butter.

'Crooked Jake'
Freddie Windsor

When Freddie came to stay at home for Easter, my mother firmly told him that none of the family ever ate Easter eggs. For the next week, we wondered why our guest seemed to eat very little at meals. After he left, we discovered piles of giant Easter egg wrappers hidden under his bed. Freddie had spent the week pigging out on his own.

1 glass milk (skimmed)
2 measures brandy
1 tablespoon Nesquik
1 sprinkling nutmeg

This cocktail is best prepared IN BULK (see below), but beware: the slightest deviation from the pursuant instructions is guaranteed to result in serious injury and / or death.

Ensure you are alone in the house and lock noisy pets away. Disconnect all phones and advance menacingly into the kitchen.

Take your time in choosing the right glass, remembering you only get one chance with this baby. Remove the dust and cobwebs from your box of Nesquik and save for later. Choose your largest, toughest mixing-bowl and empty the powder into it until the bowl is approximately one-third full; then gently frotter the grains with your fingers. You are now ready to move on to the next stage: the brandy. Splatter the Nesquik with the liquid until you have a viscous brown glue not unlike dried blood, and whisk vigorously. Next scoop half a tablespoon of the matter into your glass (this is the equivalent of two measures brandy and one tablespoon Nesquik as above), and add milk. Stir carefully and leave to settle. Exactly four minutes later plunge a sharp knife into the glass to disperse any undissolved Nesquik, and sprinkle with nutmeg.

Drink immediately in one gulp and repeat process as required.

Best Mushrooms
Lily Balfour

The second I met Lil, aged eleven, I was entranced.

Chop up a handful of any sort of mushrooms you can lay your hands on, I like Portobello ones. Cook them in some butter, add a couple of spoonfuls of double cream and a great handful of gruyere cheese. Stir until it has melted. Put it in either several little ramekins or one great dish and sprinkle more gruyere on top, grill and eat immediately.

Sweet Potato
Ella Windsor

I am not mad about coconut but will trust Ella when she says that this is delicious as everything else she has cooked me has always been wonderful.

Sweet potatoes, coconut shavings, butter, a fork.

Cut open the sweet potatoes and mash surface around a bit with fork. Put some butter on top to seep in fork grooves. Sprinkle coconut shavings on top. Place both halves on baking tray. Bake for thirty minutes.

For some reason it's delicious.

PUDDINGS

The Best Chocolate Pudding in the World
Isobel Wood

One of my greatest friends, who does not relish hours in the kitchen, often cooks this wonderful and most sweet tempered pudding which she was given by her mother-in-law. It has never, ever let me down, and I can never, ever make enough.

8oz dark cooking chocolate
4 oz butter
8 oz soft brown sugar
4 tbsp plain flour
6 eggs

Melt chocolate, butter and sugar and stir in the flour and the egg yolks. Now beat the egg whites until stiff and fold into the mixture. This can now be left for up to an hour. Now pour into a large oblong, flat, china dish and bake in a hot oven for ten minutes. Serve with lots of thick cream and don't think of counting the calories.

Orange and Lavender Panacotta
Hacienda San Rafael

We spent part of our honeymoon here and I was in seventh heaven as the food, like everything else, was faultless.

600ml double cream
150ml milk
2 tbs glucose
250g caster sugar
2 grated oranges
1 tps lavender leaves
3 gelatine leaves

Place the cream, milk and sugar into a large saucepan, and with the orange zest bring to the boil and reduce by one third and remove from the heat.
Throw in the lavender leaves and leave to infuse.
During this process soak the gelatine in warm water until it becomes solidified.
Remove and squeeze the excess water, add to the mixture and stir until fully dissolved.
Once this process has been completed, strain through a fine sieve and allow the mixture to cool. Once cool, pour the mixture into your dariole moulds to about half way and then place in fridge to set.

Lavender

144

American Blueberry Pudding
Drusilla Fraser

This is INCREDIBLE!

(6-8 people)

Blueberries
Butter
Sugar
Bread (cut into small square croutons)

Heat up in a large flying pan 2-3 oz. butter, when foaming add small white bread croutons and when they are golden brown add two tablespoons brown Demerara or caster sugar. Cook for a minute, shuggling the pan and empty two packs of blueberries and cook for a further minute until the fruit starts splitting. Put in warmed dish and serve with whipped cream.

Yum yum.

Lemon Haze
Archbishop Conti

4 eggs, separated
2 lemons
Lemon jelly
7½ teaspoons caster sugar

Beat yolks and sugar together until light and fluffy. Melt jelly in a quarter pint of water. Grate rind of lemons, squeeze the juice and combine with jelly. When cold add to yolk and sugar. Whisk whites and fold into jelly and yolk mixture. Pour into a large glass dish or individual ones. Decorate with cream when set.

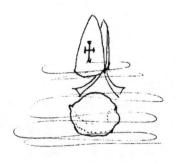

Lemon Haze.

Tiramisù (Pick-me-up)
William Gibbs

Gibbo is a jolly creature and I am absolutely thrilled that he has given me this recipe.

Serves 8

8 eggs
700g mascarpone
6 tablespoons sugar
2 packets Savoiardi biscuits (or sponge fingers if not available)
5 cups strong espresso coffee
Brandy / Amaretto to taste
Cocoa (unsweetened) to decorate

Prepare the espresso coffee and put in flat dish to cool. Add brandy.

Carefully separate the yolks from the whites. Mix the egg yolks and sugar together until pale yellow (almost white) in colour. Mix in the mascarpone. Beat egg whites until they form stiff peaks. Fold egg whites into mascarpone mixture.

Take a large dish (at least 5 cm in height and 25 cm diameter) and dip each sponge finger in the coffee mixture. Cover base of dish with sponge fingers. Cover with a layer of the mascarpone mixture. Add another layer of sponge fingers dipped in coffee mixture. Cover with remainder of mascarpone mixture (should hide all sponge fingers). Sprinkle cocoa on top as desired. Cover dish with cling film and put in fridge for at least four hours.

Serve – buon appetito!

Caramelised Apple with Filo Crisps and Date and Apple Puree
The Duchess of Westminster

1 vanilla pod
Zest and juice ½ lemon
Juice ½ orange
125g butter
200g pack filo pastry
7 crisp apple ie Cox's or Braeburn
3 tbsp honey
2tbsp calvados or brandy
250g medjool dates, stoned
125g caster sugar
125ml crème fraiche or vanilla ice cream

Making the citrus butter:
Put the lemon zest and the two juices together in a pan and add 25g butter. Heat it up until the butter has melted. This is to butter the sheets of filo pastry and make them stick together. It also gives the pastry more flavour.

Making the filo squares:
Heat the oven to 200°C
Count how many sheets there are, then you can work out how many sheets you need to give you 54 8cmx8cm squares.

Cut the squares out. Don't forget to wrap the pastry you are not using in a damp tea towel or cling film to stop it drying out.

Peel off one of the squares and brush it with the citrus butter. Do this with two more sheets so that it is three sheets thick. Place on a baking try and repeat with all the other squares.

You need the pastry to be as flat as possible so a good tip is to place another baking sheet the same size as the one the pastry is on, on top of the sheets, then put them in the oven for about eight minutes until golden.

(continued...)

Cooking the apples:
Peel six apples then cut them in half through the centre so that they are still a round shape. Take out the core and seeds.
Melt the rest of the butter in a pan and add the honey. Bring to the boil, then add the apples. Spoon the syrup over the apples and turn them over occasionally. It will take about ten minutes until the apples are cooked. Pour in the calvados or brandy. Spoon it over the apples until they are a rich golden colour.

Making the date purée:
Chop the dates roughly, then peel and core the last apple. Chop up the apple and place in the pan with the dates.
Add 100ml of water and simmer until the apple has cooked and the dates are soft.
Put in a food processor to make a smooth purée.

Making the caramel:
Put the sugar and two tablespoons of water into a heavy based pan.
Cook on a high heat until the sugar turns a golden colour.

Putting it all together:
Warm up the date purée and put in a small piping bag with a plain nozzle.
Pipe small mounds of purée onto the plates.
Next put a layer of pastry in the middle of the plate and spread with a little date purée.
Place a warm apple half on top.
Place another filo square to top of the apple. You will have enough pastry and apple to make another layer on top of this, but one layer is probably enough.

Serving it:
Pour the caramel around the plates and serve with vanilla ice cream or crème fraiche.

Chocolate Roulade
Lucy Carr Ellison

This recipe is reason enough to own this cookbook.

8 eggs
275g caster sugar
350g good chocolate

Melt chocolate in large glass bowl over gently simmering water... separate eggs and add sugar to egg yolks until creamy. Beat whites until soft peak stage and then, having allowed melted chocolate to cool, add to egg yolks and fold in egg whites.

Pour into a lined shallow baking dish (any dish will do I have even made it in a roasting dish!) and place in oven at 180 degrees (bottom shelf of Aga) ...after 10 minutes check mixture with skewer...if it comes out clean hey presto!

Place damp dish cloth over pudding and let it rest over night.
Next day melt 100 grams of best dark chocolate – whip up cream and add a bit of icing sugar. Remove dish cloth and pour roulade onto baking parchment lightly dusted with icing sugar. Spread over the chocolate and carefully cover with cream...and roll up gently.

Delicious.

Tarte Tatin
Tiggie Hoare

Serves 6

100g granulated sugar
20g butter
1kg of apples
Enough short crust pastry to cover an 18-20cm diameter mould!

Cook the sugar in a pan over a high heat with three tablespoons of water. When it is a runny caramel, pour it into the bottom of a round mould (tart tin) of 18-20cm diameter.

Peel and core the apples and cut them into quarters. Arrange them in a circle in the tin over the cooled caramel. Sprinkle a tablespoon of sugar over the top of the apples. Cut the butter into little pieces and distribute over apples also.

Roll out the pastry until it is about 4mm thick and lay it over the apples. Press the pastry down lightly.

Cook the tarte in the oven at 230°C for about 20-30 minutes. The pastry should turn a golden colour.

To take the tarte tatin out of the mould, put a plate over the top while it is still hot from the oven, and turn over.

Passion Fruit Pavlova
Alice Lutyens

One meringue nest per person (M&S meringue nests are the best, they have nothing but egg whites and sugar in them)

One ripe passion fruit per person (it should be rather wrinkled and black)

One large scoop whipped cream per person

Put the nest on a plate, smooth the cream over it, then squeeze the passion fruit all over including the seeds.

Sussex Pond Pudding
The Countess De La Warr

Anne lives in the beautiful hills of Sussex in what is by far my favourite village in England and I make an annual pilgrimage for the village fete, which makes Little Britain *look like a documentary rather than a comedy. She is the champion breeder of Shetland ponies which roam the hills around her home in tiny fluffy packs.*

Half a pound of plain flour
Half an ounce of baking powder
Three ounces of suet
Five fluid ounces of water
Pinch of salt
Three ounces of currants
Four ounces of butter
Five ounces of brown sugar

Mix butter and sugar together. Mix the rest as in suet pudding. Put the suet mix in a basin with the butter / sugar mix in the middle, cover the top with suet mix and over with foil and steam for about two hours. This is a very popular nursery / shooting lunch pudding for winter.

Downside Delight
Father Philip Jebb

Father Philip took part in my marriage and despite calling me Carol during the vows, he remains one of the most fascinating men I have ever met. He lives in Downside Abbey, one of England's greatest monasteries and embodies all the most wonderful qualities of a life dedicated to God, including a keen appreciation of good food. This recipe has been served to the monks at Downside for countless years and is one of their favourites.

3 cooking apples
½lb of apricot jam
2 eggs
¾ pint of milk
Flaked almonds

Take a 12" quiche dish and lay the peeled slices of apples over the whole.

Spread the jam onto the apple

Beat the eggs with the milk and pour this onto the apples and jam.

Throw flaked almonds over the whole thing, lots of them.

Cook at 174°C for thirty minutes or until the apple is soft the almonds on top are crispy.

A little cream will ease it down, though it is not necessary.

Coffee Rousse
Mrs Raoul Lempriere Robin

4 oz butter
4 oz sugar
3 yolks
Cup of coffee
Sponge cake
Cream

Cream butter, add sugar, stir well. Add yolks stir well. Slowly add coffee and stir well, add as much as possible. Line pudding bowl with grease proof paper and put alternative layers of sponge cake and coffee mixture plus coffee so that the whole pudding is moist. Fill basin an leave in the fridge all night. Turn pudding out and cover with cream.

Damson Cream Pot
Jules Blackwell

Jules is a masterchef who lives in Lancashire. She keeps tarantulas in the sitting room which always fascinated us when we were growing up. We rushed to see Molly in her tank whenever we went there.

1 pint of (sweetened to taste) damson purée with stones removed
6 egg yolks
¾ pint double cream
3 tablespoons damson gin

Preheat the oven to 140°C. Put all the ingredients in a blender and pass through a sieve. Pour into individual ramekins and cook in a bain marie in the oven for about an hour. The creams should still wobble a little when ready – remember that they will carry on cooking a little after they have been removed from the oven. Leave to cool and then chill overnight. Serve with more damson gin to just cover the surface and cold pouring cream.

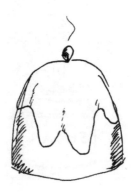

Chocolate Tart
Vanessa Reid

Vanessa Rocks.

3 eggs
3 egg yolks
200g dark chocolate
50g caster sugar

Place the eggs and sugar in a mixer and whisk until a creamy consistency.

Meanwhile put the chocolate in a glass bowl and place over a bain-marie until fully melted.

Pour over the egg mixture and beat until smooth then pour into tart case and bake for ten minutes at 150°C.

Serve with Banana Ice Cream (*see page 158*)

Banana Ice Cream
Nick Devereux

Nick is an exceptionally good artist whose paintings will hang in the finest galleries of Europe in years to come, I have no doubt whatsoever.

250ml double cream
250ml milk
125g caster sugar
3 bananas
5 egg yolks
Juice of 1 lemon

Put the cream and milk into a saucepan and place over a low heat.

Chop the bananas finely and add to the creamy mixture and simmer until the banana has softened, then blitz in a liquidizer until smooth.

Meanwhile beat the egg yolks and sugar until creamy, then pour over the banana mixture, mix well, pour back into the saucepan and put back on the heat and stir until it reaches a custard consistency.

Add lemon juice, then strain through a fine sieve and cool.

Once cooled it is ready to put through the ice cream maker.

Especially good on Chocolate Tart (*see page 157*)

Butterscotch Sauce
Will Buckhurst

Bucky is one of my favourite people and my son's godfather. He has a fantastic sense of humour and is a rare species.

2 oz butter
3 oz soft brown sugar
5 oz golden syrup
4 oz double cream
Vanilla essence

Put all the ingredients in a saucepan and heat gently until sugar and butter dissolve, bring to the boil and simmer for 3/5 minutes. Serve warm, will keep in fridge for a few days. This is excellent on ice cream, poached pears/apples or as a topping for sponge based puddings.

Croissant and Butter Pudding
Zara Noel

6 croissants
A handful of sultanas
250ml cream
1 vanilla pod / a few drops of vanilla essence
3 small egg yolks
½ a table spoon of cornflower

Start by preparing six ramekins on a deep baking tray, the ramekins should be generously greased with an old butter packet.

Next rip the croissants into small pieces and place in the ramekins along with the sultanas. Don't squash down the croissants as the custard will need to be able to get around the bits of croissant to combine. Heat the cream and vanilla pod gently on the hob, do not let it boil.

While the cream is warming, whisk three small egg yolks with half a tablespoon of cornflower. The eggs act as a thickening agent in the custard and the cornflower stabilises the eggs and stops them curdling. Whisk the eggs for approximately two minutes.

Take the cream off the heat and slowly pour into egg yolks whilst whisking.

Once all the cream has gone into the egg yolks, put back on the heat and stir until the custard has thickened.

Take the custard off the heat and pour into the ramekins over the croissants until it reaches the top of the ramekins.
Pour some water into the deep baking tray which the ramekins are sitting in. The water should reach about a quarter of the way up the ramekins. This is known as a Bain Marie.

(continued...)

Put in the oven for twenty minutes at 180°C.

Take the ramekins out of the Bain Marie and put a knife around the edges of each one to loosen.

Next turn the ramekins upside down on a small side plate and if all goes according to plan they should come free from the ramekins!

Serve with some vanilla ice cream or a fruit coulis sauce.

This recipe is very versatile and can be made with pain au chocolat for chocoholics.

Marmalade Ice Cream
Campbell's of Beauly

This shop is a beacon for anyone visiting the Highlands. It is the finest tweed shop you will ever hope to find run by three charming siblings.

8 egg yolks
8 oz caster sugar
1 pint double cream
½ jar marmalade

Whip egg yolks and sugar until light and fluffy. Whip double cream. Mix all ingredients together and freeze.

Banana Yoghurt
Raoul Fraser

My beloved brother works like a dog in the city and returns home too late at night to spend time in the kitchen on his supper. He can knock this up in a matter of seconds. It is perfect as a pudding for supper if you divide the mixture up into individual ramekins.

Chop up a banana.

Pile delicious plain yoghurt on top (I prefer Yeo Valley's).

Sprinkle muscavado sugar all over.

Pop in the fridge for thirty minutes or however long to make your life easier. Could not be more delicious.

Sticky Toffee Pudding
Kurt Trinder, The Duke of Cumberland's Head

The Duke of Cumberland's Head, in Clifton, Oxfordshire, is one of the most comfortable pubs in the country, and it is famous for this delicious pudding.

250 g stoned dates
1/2 pint water
1/2 teaspoon bicarbonate of soda
8 oz butter
8 oz caster sugar
2 eggs
8 oz self-raising flour
4 oz brown sugar
6 fl oz double cream
4 tbsp golden syrup

Place water, dates and bicarbonate of soda in a pan. Bring to the boil, then reduce the heat and simmer for five minutes.

In a bowl, cream together the sugar and butter. Gradually add the eggs, adding a little flour if the mixture starts to split.

Add the rest of the flour and slowly beat in the date mixture.

Place in an oven proof dish and bake for thirty minutes. Insert a knife into the sponge, if it comes out clean, it is ready, if it comes out with baking mixture still on it, leave for a few more minutes.

Place the sugar, golden syrup and cream in a saucepan. Bring to the boil, reduce heat and simmer for about five minutes. When ready, pour over the sponge.

Wow.

TEA-TIME

Portavo Biscuits
Dave Ker

Dave has always inspired me to eat more! He says the biscuits are sensational.

3 oz Lurpack
2oz plain flour
3 oz caster sugar
3 oz nibbed almonds

Cream butter and sugar until very light and fluffy. Add flour and stir in almonds. Bake teaspoonfuls on a greased tin at 200°C, set well apart, as they come out quite flat and like a brandy snap.

Allow to cool on tray until moveable onto a cake rack to cool fully.

Flapjacks
The Countess De La Warr

I've often eaten these in the kitchen of Buckhurst Park, surrounded by animals, while gazing out the window at the tumbling pigeons.

6oz rolled oats
3oz butter
4 oz sugar
1 desertspoon golden syrup

Melt fat and syrup in a saucepan, add oats and sugar, stir until sugar dissolves, put mixture in a greased cake tin and cook in a hot oven for twenty minutes. Allow to cool, cut into fingers and cool further before turning out.

Brownies
Jamie Grimston

I very fortunately ate these incredible brownies just before the book went to print. I know that everyone has a brownie recipe but this really is the definitive, I cannot describe how good they are.

4oz plain chocolate
2oz milk chocolate
10 oz light muscavado sugar
6 oz butter
4 oz self raising flour
3 eggs beaten
4 oz pecan nuts – toasted
1 tbs cocoa powder
1 tsp baking powder

Melt the butter, two kinds of chocolate and muscavado sugar over a gentle heat stirring until melted. Remove from the heat.

Add the beaten eggs then flour, cocoa powder and baking powder. Fold in until just incorporated, don't beat. Pour into an 8" x 8" and 1½" deep tin lined with baking parchment and cook in a preheated oven (160°C) for 30 minutes.

Leave in the tin to cool then cut into squares (I use Green and Black's chocolate and cocoa powder).

Anzac Biscuits
Philippa Holland

Philippa's pink doorway is always open.

4oz butter
1 tablespoon golden syrup
2 tablespoons boiling water
1½ teaspoons bicarbonate of soda
1 cup of rolled oats
¾ cup coconut
1 cup of plain flour
1 cup sugar

Melt the butter and golden syrup over a gentle heat, add mixed boiling water and bicarbonate of soda. Pour into dry ingredients.

Mix well.

Drop teaspoonful of mixture on greased tray.

Bake in slow oven (300°F) for twenty minutes.

Cool on tray for a few minutes, remove and store in an airtight container when cool.

Makes about 4 dozen.

Chocolate Crunch Cake
Michael Dooley

Mr Dooley is the kindest Doctor you will ever find. He wrote: 'I have got a very sweet tooth and I remember, as a child, my parents having tea parties in Wimbledon. I used to wait anxiously until they moved from the dining room into the sitting room in anticipation that they would leave some Chocolate Crunch cake behind. Sadly, due to the excellent cooking of my mother, this was never the case.'

12 oz plain dessert chocolate
4 oz butter
1 large can condensed milk
10 oz rich tea biscuits crushed
4 oz cherries chopped, or 1oz raisins and 6 walnut halves chopped

Melt chocolate, butter and milk together. Add biscuits and fruit and pack into foil lined baking tray. Chill for three hours or put in freezer. Turn out when set. Extra melted chocolate can be poured over the cake if you wish.

Serves 8-10

Lemon Ice Cake
Lady Lang

4oz butter
2 eggs
6oz self raising flour
6oz caster sugar
Grated rind of lemon

Oil 7" cake tin and line base.

Whizz all ingredients. Put in tin and bake for fifty minutes at 175°C.

Remove from oven and leave in tin.

Icing:
4 oz of granulated sugar
Juice of 1 lemon

Mix together and spoon over hot cake.
Leave until cold before turning out.
Freezes well.

Kaiserschmarrn
Rachael Hall

Kaiserschmarrn has been eaten in Austria since the dawn of time by hungry skiers. It makes the lightest, fluffiest pancakes and is adored by one and all who eat them.

100g plain flour
120ml full milk
2 beaten egg yolks
2 egg whites whisked
50g caster sugar
25g raisins
Icing sugar

For the plum jam:
200g plums
400ml orange juice
50ml lemon juice
30g sugar
Cornflour
Cinnamon and nutmeg to taste

For the jam: simmer all the ingredients together on a low heat until the plums are soft. Thicken with some cornflour (mixed with a little hot water). Add some cinnamon and nutmeg to taste, and keep the jam warm.

For the pancake: mix the milk, flour, egg yolks and half of the caster sugar into a paste, so that it is smooth. Beat the egg whites and the rest of the caster sugar separately until thick, then stir into the paste. Prepare a frying pan with lots of melted butter and pour in the mixture, and sprinkle with raisins. Cook the pancake on both sides, until very crispy and golden brown.

To serve, break up the crispy pancake into small pieces and sprinkle with icing sugar. Serve together with the jam on warm plates.

Wheat Free Chocolate Cake
Lulu Stoffel

I can still remember the first time I ate this cake. It was rather embarrassing as it had been given as a birthday cake to a friend during a house party. I spent all weekend rushing into the pantry to eat it and devoured nearly all of it myself, leaving the poor birthday boy puzzled as to its whereabouts.

250 grams ground almonds
250 grams sugar
6 eggs
120g dark cooking chocolate, Menier is a good one
150g butter

Cream the butter and sugar. Add the egg yolks and mix in well. Then add the almonds.

Melt the chocolate with two tablespoons of water on a very low heat. Gradually add the melted chocolate to the mixture.

Fold in the stiff egg white mixture. Bake in a preheated oven for 45 minutes on the middle shelf at 180°C.

Leave to cool completely.

For the icing :
50g butter
100g dark cooking chocolate
4 tablespoons of water.

Spread all over the cake.

Chocolate Biscuit Cake
Jemma Phipps

Jemma is Auntie Ponnie's Granddaughter and when not painting a masterpiece she makes this following the same recipe that she has used since she was eight years old.

1lb rich tea biscuits
8oz butter
6 rounded tablespoons cocoa powder
4 rounded tablespoons caster sugar
2 heaped tablespoons golden syrup
8oz plain chocolate

Cut biscuits up.
Melt butter, sugar syrup and cocoa in a saucepan on a low heat. Stir until blended. Throw in the chopped up biscuits and turn over mixture until all are covered. Spoon mixture into cake tin (ready buttered) and press down mix.
Melt the plain chocolate in a bowl over a saucepan of boiling water and pour over biscuit mixture and spread evenly. Put in fridge to chill and firm then eat!

Russian Toffee
Phillippa Holland

1 tin condensed milk
4 teacups sugar
2 tablespoons golden syrup
6oz butter
½ teaspoon vanilla essence

In a large saucepan melt the butter and sugar. Add milk and syrup.
Bring gently to the boil and boil slowly for twenty minutes, stirring all the time with a wooden spoon.
Put a little of the toffee into some cold water and check to see that a soft ball is formed.
Flavour with vanilla essence before removing from the heat.
Pour into a greased swiss roll tin. Make sure that it is cut into squares when setting.

Banana Cake
Sarah Keswick

4oz butter
10oz caster sugar
2 eggs beaten
12oz self raising flour
½ tsp baking powder
½ tsp bicarbonate of soda
½ tsp salt
5 ripe bananas
1 tsp vanilla essence
3 floz butter milk
¾ pint double cream whipped
2 tbsp lemon juice

Grease the bottom and sides of two deep 20 cm (8 inch) sandwich tins and dust them with a little flour.

Put the butter in a bowl and cream it with the sugar until the mixture is light and fluffy, then add the beaten eggs a little at a time. Beat well after each addition. Sift together the self raising flour, baking powder, bicarbonate of soda and salt. Fold the dry ingredients into the creamed mixture and blend well.

Mash three of the bananas and stir in the vanilla essence and buttermilk until mixed. Gradually beat the banana mixture into the cake mixture.

Divide the cake mixture between the tins and bake at 180°C / 350°F for about thirty minutes or until well risen and firm.

Cool in the tins on a wire rack for a short time, then turn on to the rack to cool completely.

When the cake layers are cold, sandwich them together and coat top and sides with cream.

Slice the remaining bananas, dip in lemon juice and use to decorate the top of the cake.*

* We never bother with that bit.

Love Bug Cake
Philippa Holland

250g wholewheat flour
2 teaspoon baking powder
1 teaspoon ground mixed spice
2 teaspoons ground cinnamon
3 tablespoons soya flour
6 tablespoons water
175g soft brown sugar
50g pecan nuts or walnuts
1 large very ripe banana
50g dried figs
25g sultanas
1 tablespoon lime marmalade
150g carrots
175ml oil

Icing:
200g creamed coconut
About 75ml hot water
Grated rind of half an orange
3-4 tablespoons icing sugar
3 tablespoons orange juice
100g lightly tasted desiccated coconut

Preheat the oven to 190°C / 375°F. Grease and base line a 20cm round cake tin.

Combine the wholewheat flour, baking powder and spices in a large mixing bowl. Mix the soya flour and water and stir into the bowl with the sugar and nuts. Mash the banana and add it the figs, sultana's, marmalade, carrots and oil. Mix thoroughly.
Transfer the mixture to the prepared tin and level the top. Bake in the oven for 40-50 minutes or until firm to the touch. Leave to cool in the tin. Remove.

(continued...)

Mash the creamed coconut with some of the hot water, using a fork then beat in the orange rind, icing sugar and orange juice with enough hot water to give the mixture a smooth consistency for spreading on top and sides of the cake. Sprinkle coconut all over.

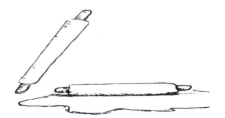

Spice Cake (Piernik)
Danuta Mazur

4 cups honey
5 eggs
4 cups flour
1 tsp baking soda
1 cup almonds
1 cup citron
2 tbs finely chopped orange peel
¼ tsp ground cloves
½ tsp cinnamon

Heat honey until it darkens. When cool, add egg yolks one at a time and continue creaming. Sift in flour and baking soda and mix thoroughly. Add almonds, citron and other ingredients, increasing amounts if a more spicy taste is preferred. Fold in stiffly beaten egg whites. Pout into well greased mould dusted with flour and bake in slow oven for an hour.

Savannah and Moses' Fussy Eaters Banana Bread
Savannah Miller

I kept to a wheat free diet for the last few months of my first pregnancy and could not have survived without this cake. Something that you can always serve with confidence when you have guests who are watching their waistlines.

175g Flour (½ cornflour, ½ rice flour)
125g butter
300g banana ripened
4 tablespoons honey
½ tsp bicarbonate of soda
2 tsp baking powder
2 eggs

Melt butter, wait till cool. Whizz up the eggs, honey, and mashed banana. Slowly add the dry ingredients bit by bit till you get a cake consistency. Line a loaf tin and cook at 180°C until ready.

Scones
Diana Hepburn

Diana is our much adored Nanny who made us the sort of teas that will live in a child's memory forever.

1oz caster sugar
8oz flour
1oz baking powder
2oz butter
¼ pint milk
(optional extra is 1 oz of fruit, such as raisins)

Rub in butter to the flour, add the sugar, baking powder and milk a little at a time. Roll out the mixture and cut out circles, place on a buttered baking tray. Pop into a hot oven, perhaps 220°C for about ten minutes until they have risen and slightly browned on top. Eat immediately.

To make cheese scones, delete the sugar from the ingredients and replace with 4oz of cheese and follow recipe as usual.

INDEX

Notes

Notes

Notes

Notes

Temperature Guide

Because different people are used to different means of judging temperature, the following guide gives a useful comparison between gas mark, celsius, and farenheit.

Heat	Gas Mark	°Farenheit	°Celsius
Cool / Very Slow Cook	½	250	120
Warm / Slow Cook	2	300	150
Moderate	4	350	175
Moderately Hot	5	375	190
Hot	7	425	220
Very Hot	8	450	230
Extremely Hot	9	475	250